Praise for *Surrendered*

In this study, you'll be learning from a friend who is familiar with the painful parts of life and a guide who has traveled the hard road of surrender. She won't lead you astray; she'll lead you straight to the heart of God.

—**Tiffany Bluhm,** speaker, podcaster, and author of *She Dreams*

Surrendered is the antidote for women like me who struggle with the dreaded c-word, control. Through rich biblical teaching, vulnerable personal stories, and gentle (but insistent) beckoning, Barb Roose leads us to a new place of freedom through trust in God. Finally...we can learn to release our white-knuckled grip and rest.

—**Amy Carroll,** Proverbs 31 Ministries speaker and writer, author of *Breaking Up with Perfect* and *Exhale*

With clear biblical insights and practical steps, Barb helps us envision the freedom available to us and then walk into that freedom. I highly recommend this study to anyone feeling stuck or needing a breakthrough in any area of their life (which is all of us!).

—**Deb Gruelle,** best-selling author and speaker

Barb speaks as a wise Bible teacher and as a friend who fully understands the deepest places of hurt in your heart. I am so thankful for this study that not only leads women to God's peace, power, and provision but also offers a guide who holds your hand as you walk together

.—**Katy McCown,** Proverbs 31 writer and founder of And She Laughs Ministries

In this six-week journey of *Surrendered*, we will learn six key principles of relinquishing and receiving with Barb Roose as our dynamic guide through personal story, in-depth exposition, and contagious passion. Dive in for faith and freedom!

—**Lucinda Secrest McDowell,** author of *Soul Strong* and *Dwelling Places*

Barb's surrender principles free us from the need to control others and from anger or frustration over life's disappointing and hurtful circumstances. As a Bible study teacher, I highly recommend this study.

—**Janet Holm McHenry,** best-selling author of twenty-four books including *Prayer-Walk* and *The Compete Guide to the Prayers of Jesus*

As a Christian counselor, I often see women struggling with fear and anxiety with circumstances beyond their control. Surrendered *provides biblical and practical ways to escape the fight, flight, or freeze traps that seem almost unavoidable in our world today.*

—**Michelle Nietert,** clinical director, Community Counseling Associates

This study is full of transformative principles to free you from the grip of control. Whether you are tempted to flee difficult circumstances, fix outcomes, or force your way forward, Barb lays out a clear path to experience God's lasting peace, power, and provision as you live surrendered to Him.

—**Katie M. Reid,** author of *Made Like Martha*, Bible teacher, and host of The Martha + Mary Show podcast

With vivid storytelling and deep study of Scripture, Surrendered *offers a shame-free, practical, and hope-filled journey through struggles and into life. This study provides a toolkit for life in our inevitable wildernesses.*

—**Jane Rubietta,** speaker and award-winning author of *Heartbreak of a Mother, Finding Your Dream*, and many other titles

When facing tough times one of the hardest things to figure out is what to hold on to and what to let go. If you need help, this study is for you. May its words give you the grace to surrender your all to One who rescues those in the midst of trouble.

—**Susan Seay**, speaker and author of *The Intentional Parent: Parenting on Purpose When Life Gets Busy*

Barb gently leads us to the core truths about Christ and His character. She has a gift for shining light on who God is—and because of who He is, how we can live freely surrendered to the Spirit's leading.

—**Amy Seiffert,** speaker and author of *Grace Looks Good on You*

Barb is a fellow struggler and overcomer who gets down on her knees with you and jumps for joy when you win, sharing freely how God has helped her win in so many of life's difficulties. She gets it. She lives it. This is a study for every woman who knows pain and wants peace.

—**Tami Ward**, Central Women's Pastor, Discovery Church, Orlando, Florida

A STUDY *of* JESUS *in the* WILDERNESS

Surrendered

Letting Go & Living Like Jesus

BARB ROOSE

Abingdon Women/Nashville

Surrendered

Letting Go and Living Like Jesus

Copyright © 2020 Abingdon Press
All rights reserved.

ISBN 978-1-5018-9628-6

20 21 22 23 24 25 26 27 28 29 — 10 9 8 7 6 5 4 3 2 1
MANUFACTURED IN THE UNITED STATES OF AMERICA

To my Jesus-loving sister with the weary soul,
you are not alone in your struggle.
God knows the weight that you carry.
He hears the cry of your heart.
You are seen. Most of all,
you are dearly loved.

Contents

About the Author

Barb Roose is a popular speaker and author who is passionate about connecting women to one another and to God, and helping them apply the truths of God's Word to the practical realities and challenges they face as women in today's culture. Barb enjoys teaching and encouraging women at conferences and events across the country, as well as internationally. She is the author of the Bible studies *I'm Waiting, God: Finding Blessing in God's Delays*; *Joshua: Winning the Worry Battle*; and *Beautiful Already: Reclaiming God's Perspective on Beauty* and the books *Winning the Worry Battle: Life Lessons from the Book of Joshua* and *Enough Already: Winning Your Ugly Struggle with Beauty*. She also writes a regular blog at BarbRoose.com and hosts the "Better Together" podcast. Previously Barb was executive director of ministry at CedarCreek Church in Perrysburg, Ohio, where she served on staff for fourteen years and co-led the annual Fabulous Women's Conference that reached more than ten thousand women over five years. Barb is the proud mother of three adult daughters and lives in Northwest Ohio.

Follow Barb:

 @barbroose

 @barbroose

 Facebook.com/barbararoose

Blog   BarbRoose.com (check here for event dates and booking information)

Introduction

Does your life feel like more than you can handle right now?

Take a deep breath, friend. It's okay to not be okay right now. The good news is that God has a better way for you to get through whatever it is that you're going through.

Perhaps you picked up this study because you or someone you love is in the midst of a difficult struggle. There's something or someone in your life that you're worried about, and while you know that you can't change it, that hasn't stopped you from trying. And after all of your begging, pleading, paying, and praying, you're worn out. Not just tired, but your heart may resemble a raggedy blanket, shredded and torn over and over again. Yet there's still that little determined fire within you that desperately longs to fix what's broken.

Our natural desire is to protect ourselves and what we love, fix what's broken, and make sure that everyone and everything in our lives stays on track. Life is happy and feels good when the bills are paid, the kids make good decisions, and that last twenty pounds drops off with a few months of diet and exercise.

But what happens when life doesn't go as planned? What do you do when you can't protect yourself or what you love, fix what's broken, or prevent the future from falling off the tracks?

As much as we know that we don't have control over our circumstances, there's often this little voice in our mind that whispers, "If you work hard enough, smart enough, and long enough, you can fix this." Have you ever heard that voice? I have. And for a very long time, I believed that philosophy. In fact, there were lots of times when I didn't pray about some problems. Why pray when I didn't think that I needed God's help? For others of us, we don't want to fix as much as we just want to flee—to return to a time when things were as they used to be. We might be so busy trying to ignore the situation or escape from it that we don't take time to pray. Or we might be banging on the door of heaven with our pleas for God to stop what's happening and make everything right again.

In my own life, a situation unfolded in our family that was far beyond my ability to manage, and soon our lives spiraled out of control. The more out of control I felt, the more buttons and levers I tried to push. I worked twice as hard and devoted double the resources. I just knew that if I stuck in there long enough, I could fix all of it. However, as I kept fighting year after year, I felt mounting fear and frustration because what I loved was slipping away and I was powerless to stop it.

As a Jesus-loving woman, it was hard to acknowledge my control-loving ways. Instead, I pictured my efforts as creative or proactive problem-solving. Sadly, I ignored the possibility that I was just trying to play God in my life and the lives of others.

The moment of change for me came when I stopped being afraid to let go and trust God with whatever happened, even when God moved my life in a different or difficult direction. I finally admitted that the weight of my problems was too much for me to bear. I realized that the harder I held on, the heavier the weight became, breaking my heart over and over again. Everything changed when I decided to let go and let God carry the weight as well as work out what would come next.

Whether your tendency, like mine, is to try to control and fix problems, or you're more inclined to try to escape them or beg God to change things, the bottom line is that painful circumstances are *hard*. If you're facing a situation where you're feeling powerless, afraid, desperate, or alone, I'm glad that you're here for this *Surrendered* Bible study. As we journey together for the next six weeks, you'll have the opportunity to apply God's precious promises to the fears deep in your heart as well as learn helpful tools to reshape your attitudes and behaviors into responses that reflect how Jesus responded in difficult circumstances.

During this study, you'll follow Jesus into the Judean wilderness where He was tempted by the devil. We'll explore the wilderness as a metaphor for those long seasons of life when we face hardships and difficulties that test and challenge our faith. As we look at how Jesus faces a set of three temptations, we'll compare His responses to the Israelites, who also faced a long wilderness season centuries before. Throughout the study, you'll explore how the Israelites' lack of faith made their time in the wilderness painful; yet still they experienced God's power and blessing in their lives. Whether you're facing a long wilderness season or dealing with a difficult or destructive temptation, Jesus understands what you're going through. You are not alone. There's hope, even if today you feel like you are at the end of your rope!

If there was a word that captured Jesus' posture in the wilderness, that word would be *surrender*. Jesus didn't fight to strong-arm evil intentions or escape challenging circumstances; rather, Jesus surrendered to and flowed with God's Spirit within Him. Even in His weakened human state, Jesus stood strong against Satan, something that we'd all like to do. As we trace Jesus' footsteps in the wilderness, you'll learn from His words as well as His actions. There will be lots of reflection exercises, tools, and surrender principles for you to apply in your life.

The act of surrender is an invitation to release our problems to God and receive His provision, protection, and peace in return. The pursuit of living the surrendered life will involve allowing God to transform your head (beliefs), your heart (emotions), and your hands (actions). The goal of this study is to equip you to begin the process of letting go—which is not giving in out of fear or giving up out of discouragement, but giving over whatever you are facing to God and living each day with the faith that God is in control and the hope that God is working everything not only for your good but also the good of those you love and care about.

Surrender Principles

Learning to let go and live like Jesus isn't a switch that we can flip. Whether you're a control-loving fixer like me or someone whose tendency is to flee or escape the problem or the pain, unlearning those behaviors is a challenge. Not only do you have to evict either the "you can fix it" squatter or the "stop the pain now" bully from your mind but you also have to flood the fear-based circuitry of your heart with God's truth and promises.

One way to do this is to develop a practice of repeating a set of six surrender principles before you begin each day's study, as well as activating one or more of these principles whenever fear flows through your heart or you're tempted to flee, fix, or force situations.

1. I am not in control of others or outcomes.
2. I choose to live by faith, not rush to follow my feelings.
3. I can always let go and give my problems to God.
4. Trusting God's promises will bless me, but pushing my plans will stress me.
5. When fear tempts me to flee, fix, or force my way, I will choose to stop and pray.
6. Surrender is my only path to God's peace, power, and provision.

These principles are designed to be short but memorable. You can write them on a note card and place them in your wallet, program them into your phone, or post them anywhere as a reminder to let go and let God carry the weight for what you can't change or control.

Getting Started

Each week there are five lessons combining study of Scripture with reflection and application. As part of the study content, you'll find Extra Insights; a weekly Memory Verse; a Daily Surrender Prayer (Weeks 2–6); and short, memorable Surrender Statements to stock your *Surrendered* toolbox.

Space is provided for recording your responses and completing exercises. Throughout the study there are practical exercises that will provide you with real-time opportunities for reflection and create next-step action plans for your life, whether that might be working on a spiritual breakthrough, destroying a mental stronghold, or following through with a Spirit-led act of obedience that God may be asking you to do.

Each daily lesson should take about twenty to thirty minutes. You'll need a Bible, a pen, and an open heart that is ready to receive whatever God might speak or reveal about your surrender struggle. These lessons will help you prepare for the discussion and activities of your weekly session, if you are meeting with a group. Though you can do the study individually and reap benefits, it is designed to be done with a group for encouragement, support, and accountability. As you gather to watch the *Surrendered* DVD, you also will have the opportunity to share what you are learning and pray together.

Each video message is designed to follow and complement the content that you have studied during the week. Whether or not your group watches the video, it's so helpful to share your struggles and victories in your journey to surrender. As you do, you'll encourage one another and find strength to complete the study and put into practice all that you're learning.

A Final Word

Friend, there will always be circumstances out of our control, and the only path to God's power, peace, and provision in the midst of those circumstances is to surrender. Letting go and living like Jesus will sustain us, strengthen us, and set us up to experience God's best and beautiful blessings, not only in this life but also in the life to come.

Week 1

Waking Up in the Wilderness

(Matthew 4:1; Mark 1:12-13; Luke 4:1)

Memory Verse

[2]Consider it pure joy, my brothers and sisters, whenever you face trials of many kinds, [3]because you know that the testing of your faith produces perseverance.

(James 1:2-3)

My limp, exhausted body stretched out across my cold kitchen floor. My slippery, wet cheek pressed against the slightly sticky vinyl tile floor as tears puddled around my chin.

Moments before I was on the phone with the insurance company, begging them to cover the cost of a screening test that one of my children needed, but I couldn't afford. A company representative listened to my pleas, but ended the call after politely but firmly stating that there was no coverage for the medical test.

For several years I had feared some developmental problems and as a good mama, I wanted to find answers and someone to help me fix the problem. Instead of answers, a heavy weight of anxiety, desperation, and frustration pressed me to the floor. I hung up the phone and realized that I had no other levers to pull, no moves to make, or chips to play in trying to meet an important need in my child's life.

In addition to the fears over my daughter's development issues, I had other problems. So many problems! It seemed like changes and challenges attacked me from all sides of life. What happened to me? Only a few years back, my life felt like I'd won one of those golden tickets from *Charlie and the Chocolate Factory*. Easy years flowed around career successes, flourishing relationships, and financial security. Then, like a series of fast-falling dominoes, everything that flourished seemed to fall down or fall apart. I didn't notice at first. But as those sources of security and happiness began to disappear, I began to feel desperate and discouraged.

As I lay on my kitchen floor that day, I felt like my life was at a low as my heart fell to the ground. How *did* I *get here*? How *do* I *get out*? That day, I looked up and demanded, "God, I want my old life back!"

While I wanted to return to what I knew, God was moving my life toward His best for my life. But it meant that I'd have to let go of my plans.

Day 1: Waking Up in the Wilderness

One day you feel like you're on the top of the world. The next day it feels like the world has fallen on top of you.

No one's life is perfect. But there are times when it seems like the wind is at your back and everything is falling into place. Perhaps after years of hard work, you finally bought the house, landed the dream job, emptied the nest, or said "I do." Then, just when you finally felt like exhaling, something unexpected and shocking took your breath away. Perhaps it was a dramatic moment like finding drugs in your child's backpack, losing a job, or discovering a spouse's dishonesty.

If you've ever felt like your old life has disappeared and you're desperate to go and get it back, I'm glad that you're here.

We'll begin our study adventure by following Jesus from a spiritual mountaintop experience in His life into a period of suffering in a stark wilderness.

In His first public appearance, Jesus goes into the wilderness area where John the Baptist is preaching and asks to be baptized (Matthew 3:13). At first, John tries to talk Him out of it, but Jesus submits to baptism to set the example for His later command that believers be baptized (see Matthew 28:19-20).

Read Matthew 3:16-17. Draw a line to match each word on the left with the appropriate word(s) on the right.

Jesus — Descending like a dove

God — Baptized

Holy Spirit — Spoke from heaven

Consider the power of that moment! I don't know about you, but I would have loved to witness Jesus' baptism. During the years I served on staff at my local church, I watched thousands of baptisms, and each one moved my heart. But watching Jesus get baptized? That would be more than my mind could handle!

On top of that, imagine seeing the Spirit of God descend like a dove, landing on Jesus' head. Another holy moment! To top it all off, what would it have been like to hear God's voice from heaven express His delight in Jesus?

In this moment, it seemed like everything in Jesus' life had come together. He'd taken a faithful step of obedience and experienced the immediate presence and loving affirmation of God.

Spiritual mountaintop moments aren't the proof of God's love or favor, but they are memorable moments that remind us of a time when we felt a special connection to God.

Can you recall a spiritual mountaintop moment in your life? If you can't think of a spiritual moment, list one or two favorite moments in your life.

Some of my spiritual mountaintop moments include a powerful church camp experience in junior high when I really felt connected to God, repenting in college after a season of straying far from God, and watching my girls get baptized at different times in their childhood.

There's a reason why we refer to them as mountaintop moments because they are special moments for us to remember, but no one lives in mountaintop moments. In fact, Jesus is about to experience a dramatic change in circumstances.

In screenwriting terms, Jesus is about to experience what's called a "smash cut" where one scene transitions suddenly to another.[1]

Look up Matthew 4:1 and write out the verse below:

Then Jesus was led by the Spirit into the wilderness to be tempted there by the devil.

Read Mark 1:12-13 and Luke 4:1 in the margin. Record any additional details not mentioned in Matthew 4:1.

Being tempted by Satan
he was ā the wild animals
the angels were ministering to him
Jesus "full of the Holy Spirit"

Now that's a dramatic change!

While it's hard to pinpoint exactly where Jesus was in the wilderness, scholars believe that Jesus was in the Wilderness of Judea. This hilly area in Judah bordered the Dead Sea.[2]

Most translations of Matthew 4:1 use the word *wilderness* to describe Jesus' surroundings, but occasionally the word *desert* is used.[3] The writer Mark covers Jesus' sojourn into the wilderness in two verses. However, Mark is the only Gospel writer who makes reference to wild animals wandering around the wilderness with Jesus. Older translations refer to the animals as "wild beasts." Scholars speculate these beasts may have been animals such as bears, wolves, panthers, or even a lion.[4] While the wild animals may have represented a visible threat to Jesus, they kept to themselves.

Based on what we read in the text, the wilderness was an isolated, rugged environment away from the comforts of home. Picture a camping trip, but without any of the equipment. Camping this way is possible, but definitely not comfortable. The wilderness is described as "land not suitable for farming."[5] However, wilderness conditions did offer enough vegetation for wild animals to graze.

Examples of Spiritual Mountaintop Moments

- *Feeling a connection to God for the first time*
- *Realizing God loves you unconditionally*
- *Accepting Jesus into your heart*
- *Forgiving a long-standing hurt or offense*
- *Experiencing victory over a sin or struggle*
- *Seeing the answer to a prayer or witnessing a miracle*

[12]The Spirit immediately drove him out into the wilderness. [13]And he was in the wilderness forty days, being tempted by Satan. And he was with the wild animals, and the angels were ministering to him. (Mark 1:12-13 ESV)

And Jesus, full of the Holy Spirit, returned from the Jordan and was led by the Spirit in the wilderness. (Luke 4:1 ESV)

Based on what you read about the wilderness, describe or draw a picture of what Jesus might have seen around Him.

rocks, dirt, sand
scant vegetation
dangerous beasts
little to no water
hot sun - cold nights

The wilderness is a symbol of hardship and difficulty. In our study, you'll learn about a number of people who endured wilderness seasons such as the Israelites, Moses, Elijah, and Paul. You may have heard someone refer to a "wilderness season" or a period of time when life is hard or heartbreaking. Below I have defined some general characteristics of a spiritual wilderness. I don't know where you're at today, but if you know or realize that you're in a wilderness season, my heart is with you. As I write this study, I've been in a long wilderness season, so I'm *honored* to be walking alongside you!

A spiritual wilderness can be characterized as:

1. a long-lasting situation that seems to hit the "pause" button in your life,
2. a high-stakes situation where someone's or something's future is at risk,
3. a time when there are no quick fixes and you have little control over the timing or outcome,
4. an experience of losing satisfaction or pleasure in once pleasurable things, or
5. a season when a circumstance is causing either emotional or spiritual confusion, or both.

Is there or has there been a time period in your life that fits the definition of a spiritual wilderness? If so, what were some of the circumstances that defined your wilderness season?

Wilderness seasons are triggered by change. Do you like change? I do, but only if I'm the one in charge of making the change. When change isn't my idea, then I'm going to go kicking and screaming.

Read Matthew 4:1 again. Who led Jesus into the wilderness? Why?

The Spirit

What stands out to me in Matthew 4:1 is that the Spirit led Jesus to the wilderness. I don't know about you, but I don't like change if it's going to make my life harder. In fact, I'll fight any change that might lead to hardship or heartache. Yet Jesus went willingly. He went for a purpose so that you and I could learn how to find hope and help in our wilderness seasons.

How do you feel about change?

It's great when it feels easier. Hard to get used to when things are difficult or can be heartbreaking

In both major wilderness seasons in my adult life, the tidal wave of change has overwhelmed me. Whether I struggled against adjustments in career, shifts in personal relationships, or a transition in how I saw my personal identity, my early wilderness prayers tended to beg God to put my life back to what was familiar and comfortable.

One thing I like to remember is that when the Holy Spirit led Jesus into the wilderness, Jesus didn't go alone. Whatever it is you are facing today, you aren't facing it alone. Even if you feel abandoned right now, God is close by. Even when you feel like the weight of your fears, problems, or pain is beyond your ability to bear it, God sees you and He hasn't left you alone!

Memory Verse Reflection

At the end of Day 1 each week, you will have an opportunity to reflect on the week's Memory Verse. (For simplicity we're calling it Memory Verse, though sometimes there are one or more verses.) I have selected verses that reflect the theme of each week of study and that will uplift and encourage your heart. Here is this week's Memory Verse:

> 2-4*Consider it a sheer gift, friends, when tests and challenges come at you from all sides. You know that under pressure, your faith-life is forced into the open and shows its true colors. So don't try to get out of anything prematurely. Let it do its work so you become mature and well-developed, not deficient in any way.*
>
> (James 1:2-4 MSG)

Extra Insight

The Book of James is traditionally attributed to Jesus' brother James, who wasn't a disciple until after Jesus' resurrection. James was a leader in the Jerusalem church (see Acts 15:4-21).

What happens to our faith when we experience pressure from challenges and troubles?

I can get mad.
Turn away from God. Not feel
retired but crushed

What is the blessing that comes from being spiritually mature and well-developed (or more like Christ)?

Recognizing even hardship can
produce perseverence. Make me
better, stronger, kinder.

Going through hard seasons is tough! However, this week's Memory Verse highlights an important lesson for us to remember about how God doesn't waste any experience in our lives. Now, let's make it more personal.

Fill in the first blank with your name and the second blank with whatever you are facing:

²Consider it pure joy, ___*Carol Wade*___, whenever you face *Corona Virus, isolation. concern* *about my children, depression, anxiety* ³because you know that the testing of your faith produces perseverance.

(James 1:2-3)

Prayer

Dear God, You know that I'm facing a variety of challenges in life. Today I choose to trust that You are with me through each and every one of those challenges and that You will use them to make me more faithful and trusting of You. Amen.

Day 2: Trusting God's Heart in Hard Times

A few years ago I asked a group of people in my office to do trust falls with one another. A trust fall is where you stand with your back to another person and fall backward with the expectation that he or she will catch you. When I did this with my coworkers, there were some interesting results.

A few people, including me, managed to fall back. It felt uncomfortable to voluntarily give up control, but it was exhilarating to experience the sensation of being caught by another person. Only one person absolutely refused to participate. I appreciate this person's honest response: "Nope, I do not trust any of you to catch me."

While that response may seem harsh, there are times when I have the same attitude toward God as I'm working hard to try to fix a situation. When I'm running around trying to do everything on my own, I'm challenged to ask myself if I have trust issues with God. Why do I struggle to let go and let God deal with things?

Can you relate? *Why did I not trust God to take care of Michael?*

My definition of *trust* is having confidence that someone or something is reliable and will not fail us. When my girls ask me for help, I want them to have confidence that they can trust me and that I will do what I promised them I would do.

Do you have the confidence that God is reliable and won't fail you or those you love? This is a vital question that we wrestle with in wilderness seasons. As much as you might want to say that you trust God in hard times, you're not alone if you've secretly questioned God's heart toward you. As a wise friend bravely admitted, "I pray and I want to trust God, but in the back of my mind I wonder if He might end up giving me a whammy instead of a blessing."

When life looks and feels good, we might put aside some of our hard questions about God. But wilderness seasons put pressure on what we believe and how we live. The emotional force of long-term unemployment, a major health diagnosis, or an explosive marriage crisis pushes our belief buttons, exposing the places where we're not sure if we really believe that God is with us or for us.

When you're facing a wilderness or hard season, how do you see God? Check all that apply.

___✓___ I see God as compassionate, helpful, and loving toward me.

___✓___ I know that God loves me, but I often question whether or not He will give me the deepest desire of my heart.

_____ I want to believe that God loves me, but a lot of things have happened to make me feel otherwise.

_____ I'm afraid that God will punish me for the mistakes I've made, so I don't even expect God will want to bless me.

Other:

What are the situations when you tend to struggle to trust God?

I should trust that God will ensure my children are okay!! That I am okay... sometimes I worry I am not good enough.

Thousands of years before Christ, the Israelites left Egypt and entered the wilderness, now known as the Sinai Peninsula. After over four hundred years of slavery, the Israelites were freed in a spectacular escape through the Red Sea before entering the wilderness on a journey toward Canaan, the land God promised to them. Jesus' forty days in the wilderness mirrors the Israelites' wilderness wandering years. As we study accounts from both the Old and New Testaments over the next six weeks, we'll learn not only from Jesus' faithful example but also from some of the missteps that the Israelites made in their struggle to trust God in the wilderness. Rather than pity or even scoff at their mistakes, let's allow their experience to guide us toward faithful rather than fearful living.

Today we'll consider three insights we can gain from the Israelites' early experience in the wilderness that will help us remember God's heart toward us when life takes a turn into a wilderness season.

Read Exodus 16:1-4 and answer the following questions.

How long had the Israelites been in the wilderness?

6 weeks

What were the people complaining about?

Not having food
that they would starve

Even though the Israelites spent over four hundred years in slavery, they were ready to go back to their harsh living conditions after less than two months in the wilderness. Coincidentally, the Israelites were in an area known as the Wilderness of Sin. Hunger made them forget that God had freed them from Pharaoh, had their Egyptian neighbors give them all kinds of parting gifts, and had made possible a dramatic exit through the Red Sea. All of that was forgotten once the people got hungry, grumpy, and afraid. Suddenly, Egypt didn't seem so bad.

The people had forgotten that back in Egypt, Pharaoh had worked them mercilessly (Exodus 5:10-14) and they cried out for help (Exodus 3:7). Now they were free—though unhappy and grumpy. Yet God already had a plan to take care of them.

Read Exodus 16:4-5. How did God say that He would provide food for the Israelites? (v. 4)

It would rain down
from heaven

How much were the people to gather on the sixth day?

twice as much as usual

You may be familiar with God's provision of manna for the Israelites. In fact, God provided manna from heaven for the entire forty-year journey (Exodus 16:35), even providing for His people in the midst of their faithlessness, rebellion, and fear. This leads us to an important insight into God's heart when we find ourselves in a wilderness season.

Wilderness Insight #1: God takes care of His children at all times, including hard times.

God created a perfect world, but our sin has caused brokenness and pain. As Romans 3:23 reminds us, all of us have fallen short of God's perfect standard at one time or another. In our world, good people sin and bad things sometimes happen to good people. Wilderness seasons of hardship and heartache are a natural consequence of our fallen and sinful world.

God isn't powerless in our pain. He restores, redeems, provides, and empowers us to live through, above, and beyond our circumstances. We'll see how this unfolds as we continue to explore the Israelites' journey in the wilderness. Best of all, God's faithfulness doesn't depend on us.

While it might seem that God is rewarding the Israelites for complaining by sending manna, He's actually fulfilling the promise that He made to take care of them. God promises to take care of us, too, but how often do we get anxious because we don't trust God's heart toward us?

Jesus addresses this issue in the Sermon on the Mount.

Read Matthew 6:25-32.

What are we told not to worry about? (v. 25)

what we will eat, drink or wear

How can we know that we can trust God? (v. 26)

Look @ the birds no they don't plant or sow but God ensures they are fed. Aren't we worth more than birds?

Why does Jesus say that only pagans (nonbelievers) worry about what they will eat and drink? (vv. 31-32)

Because God already knows what we need.

"The people of Israel called the bread manna. It was white like coriander seed and tasted like wafers made with honey."

(Exodus 16:31)

No matter what season of life you are in, how has God been taking care of and providing for you?

God you have always made sure things were alright. You helped me get through school, gave me my wonderful husband + beautiful children. Things sometimes looked so bleak yet here I am. Amazing

How does Jesus' teaching challenge your questions about whether or not God will provide for you or a loved one in a challenging situation?

} *Challenges me to check my attitude when life is hard. Put my face in God*

When we're not sure if we can trust God, that's when we tend to take matters into our own hands. If we don't trust that God can rescue our children or loved ones, we're likely to twist ourselves inside out to try to save them from bad decisions or shape them into our image of who we think they should be. I spent many years of my own daughters' lives as a helicopter parent, swooping down to try to save them from bad choices or decisions.

However, there's an important lesson we can learn from the Israelites when we face hard times and insist on living our way rather than following God's way.

Read Exodus 16:16-20, and answer T (True) or F (False):

_____ *F* 1. God instructed the people to gather ~~three~~ omers per person. (v. 16)

_____ *T* 2. The Israelites followed God's directions in gathering the manna (v. 17)

_____ *T* 3. Moses instructed the people not to keep the manna overnight. (v. 19)

_____ *T* 4. Leftover manna ended up with maggots the next morning. (v. 20)

God provided manna for each day; not only that, but God also provided enough for everyone. The people didn't have to stand in the grocery store line or even pay for the food. They collected what they needed each morning for the day. This is reminiscent of Jesus' words in Matthew 6:11 when he prays, "Give us today our daily bread."

Yet there were some who didn't trust that God would provide the next day. Or maybe they figured that they would collect a little extra in case they wanted a midnight snack or God wouldn't provide enough in the future. We can have that mindset as well. This leads to the next wilderness insight.

Wilderness Insight #2: God provides what you need for today.

Here's the thing: Our attempts to fix the future often go badly. There's nothing wrong with saving for the future, unless the reason for saving is a question or fear that God won't provide.

There was a time when my obsession with planning ahead led to a lot of stockpiling and buying extra. However, a lot of waste also happened because we couldn't use all that I was buying. Then, in a wilderness season a few decades ago, I began practicing what I still call "My Principle of Daily Bread," which is, I *have enough for today. God will take care of what I need tomorrow.*

As a former obsessive planner, that wilderness season forced me to let go of trying to stockpile for the future out of fear or needing to make sure that I was comfortable. Instead, I discovered that God was a much better supplier than the grocery store—and best of all, God doesn't waste!

I love how Jesus sums this up for us:

Look up Matthew 6:34, and write it below:

So don't worry about tomorrow, for tomorrow will bring its own worries. Today's trouble is enough for today.

Again, there's nothing wrong with having life insurance, savings accounts, or retirement funds. However, Jesus doesn't want us obsessing about what God has promised to provide.

What are some of the bad outcomes or fears about tomorrow that you should stop worrying about?

money
the way I look
health (Paul's + mine)
my children's security.

Have some of your efforts been "spoiled" in the form of strained relationships or weakened health from stress or high anxiety?

Lord I have struggled so much c̄ anxiety/depression. My worries + hopes led way to frustration + over control for Michael + Amanda

Look again at Matthew 6:34. Why does Jesus say that worry about tomorrow isn't productive?

Todays trouble is enough

I am sorry

Throughout the Bible, there are many times when God instructs His people to either build memorials or keep mementos of His faithfulness to tell the story to future generations. God instructs Moses to collect a container of manna for a specific reason.

Read Exodus 16:32. Why does God want Moses to collect a jar of manna?

To preserve it so future generations could see how the Lord provided for his people.

Our memories are short! God knows that when hard times are over, we tend to forget how He got us through them. Not only would God supernaturally preserve the manna; that jar of supernatural food would be pulled out and talked about so that future generations would know God took care of His people, even though they didn't always follow Him faithfully.

Manna is a symbol and a promise of supernatural provision that we have nothing to do with. Just like the Israelites woke up each day and God provided food, so there are many places in our lives where God has provided. The question is whether or not we've been taking credit for it. Did God supernaturally provide a job at just the right time? Did you meet someone and that connection led to an unexpected blessing in your life? This leads us to today's final wilderness insight.

Wilderness Insight #3: The more you remember God's promises and provision, the less afraid you need to be in the wilderness.

Read the following verses, and match each verse to the correct description of God's character, heart, or action toward you.

"For I know the plans I have for you. They are plans for good, + not for disaster to give you a future + a hope."

Jeremiah 29:11 — God will supply all of your needs.

Jeremiah 31:1 — God gives you everything you need to live for Him.

Philippians 4:19 — God's plans for you are good, not evil.

2 Peter 1:3 — God is love.

1 John 4:8 — God will always love you.

What are one or two takeaways from today's study about God's heart toward you and whatever you're facing today?

He is always there. It's like that walk in the sand prayer!!

Prayer

God, thank You for all the times You've taken care of me during difficult seasons. As I'm thinking about all the people You've placed in my life during those times, I pray that I am also a person who helps others during their hard times. Please use me to bless and encourage someone going through a hard time today. In Jesus' name. Amen.

Day 3: Five Wilderness Trials and Three Lessons

As a kid, I looked forward to Sunday school because each week our teacher made the stories in the Bible come alive. Since we were kids, we didn't always understand what we were reading; but as we sat on those little plastic chairs in the basement of our church, our teacher used flannel board cutouts and creativity to teach us about David and Goliath, Daniel in the lions' den, and other stories. That Bible teacher was my mom. I'll never forget the day she grabbed a chair and taught us Hebrews 11:1 (KJV): "Now faith is the substance of things hoped for, the evidence of things not seen."

Mom pushed the chair before us and explained that faith is a belief or confidence we have inside when we have experience with something.

"Kids, do you believe that this chair will hold me?"

"Yes," we replied in unison.

"How do you know that this chair will hold me?"

One kid yelled: "Because we've sat in chairs before!"

While this was a very simple lesson, I've held on to what my mom taught that day—and many times afterward. She wanted us to know that we develop faith when we have experiences with God. As we get to know God better, our faith gets stronger.

The wilderness is often the perfect opportunity to get to know God better, if we're willing. We could be like the Israelites and start screaming for somebody to send us back to our old ways of thinking and living. However, if we trust God's heart toward us, perhaps we're willing to embrace this week's Memory Verse and allow the stark, simple struggle of the wilderness to expose our faith-life so that God can lead us in a new direction toward experiencing more of His promises in our lives.

Today we're going to look at five kinds of trials we face in the wilderness and three lessons or promises of God to us in those struggles. To examine these trials, we're going to look at one of the most well-known stories of hardship and heartache in the Bible, and we'll conclude by embracing Jesus' powerful promise for us that brings hope and life to our hearts no matter what kind of trial we're facing.

Read Job 1:1-12 and answer True (T) or False (F):

T Job was described as blameless and upright. (v. 1)

F He had twelve (7) sons and eight (3) daughters. (v. 2)

T Job owned a lot of animals and was the most prosperous in the East. (v. 3)

F Satan wondered why God treated Job so badly. (v. 10)

T God gave Satan permission to interfere in Job's life. (v. 12)

F Satan was allowed to kill Job. (v. 12)

In the first verse of the Book of Job, Job is described as "blameless—a man of complete integrity. He feared God and stayed away from evil" (NLT). I think we all wish that we were more like Job. However, this description of Job's life and faith is helpful because it reminds us that hardship and heartache happen to everyone, including people of faith. You may be facing a trial that comes through no fault of your own. We all face hard times, and we don't need to assign blame or fault.

In verses 9-11, Satan tells God that Job has faith only because God never lets anything bad happen to him. Satan proposes that Job would curse God's face if all that he loved and protected was taken away from him.

As we read in verse 12, God gives Satan permission to test Job with the only restriction being not to harm him physically. Job receives heartbreaking news from many messengers. It's within their messages that we can see the different kinds of trials we all face in life.

Read Job 1:14-15. What does Job hear from messenger #1?

Some came to the fields, killed the farm hands + stole all the animals

This messenger brings news that I've labeled the **Trial of Trouble**, which is upsetting or inconvenient problems in life that you can't fix.

Read Job 1:16-17. What does Job hear from messengers #2 and #3??

Burned the sheep + killed the shepherds

Chaldean raiders stole the camels + killed the servants

I've labeled the news from these messengers the **Trial of Tragedy**, which is painful circumstances arising from sudden loss, death, disaster, or evil deeds.

Read Job 1:19. What does Job hear from messenger #4?

all his children died.

Satan caused a great wind to come in from the wilderness and kill all of Job's children at once. That kind of loss is beyond comprehension. You may know what it's like to experience what I have labeled **Tornado Trial**, which is the emotional, relational, or financial collapse and devastation of the life that you once knew.

After the dust settled, Job had to choose how he would live and deal with the swirl of thoughts and emotions inside him. This happens for us, too. Every wilderness season includes a battle in which we must deal with chaotic thoughts and emotions. I have labeled this the **Trial of Turmoil**, which is our inner struggle for faith after suffering great pain and loss.

These are the four trials that happened to Job and that happen to us as well. There's one more trial, the **Trial of Temptation,** that we'll study tomorrow.

Which of these trials fits your life right now?

Trial of trouble

So, what does Job do? Imagine stopping by Job's house on that awful day and watching as Job responds to the devastating news.

Read Job 1:20-21. How does Job respond?

He grieved but did not blame God

Write verse 21 below:

"I came naked from my mother's womb and I will be naked when I leave. The Lord gave me what I had, and the Lord has taken it away. Praise the name of the Lord"

Job tears off his clothes and grabs the ancient version of a razor to shave his head. He isn't afraid to show his grief in the face of devastating suffering. The author of *The Gospel of Job* offers this observation:

Here we have a man who weeps publicly, who squirms, groans, shouts, beats his breast, a man in crippling pain who nevertheless summons the presence of mind to engage in serious conversation. Just think for a moment about this sort of behavior, and then consider the question, What sort of faith does such a man have? Regardless of what he says, regardless of all the doubts and confusion and anger that he gives vent to in words, what is it that his actions indicate?[6]

Perhaps Job's response can become an encouragement and inspiration for us, that we can praise God for what He's given us and still give thanks when what we had goes away. While God isn't the cause of our heartache, we can trust that He is the *only* one who knows how to bring good from our pain.

I don't know about you, but I never want to miss an opportunity for God to teach me a lesson or show me how to live with more strength and courage in challenging circumstances. While there are different kinds of trials, all trials can teach us three important lessons and we're going to explore those lessons now:

1. Trials teach us to WORSHIP GOD MORE.

When life is easy, our hearts may not beat as strongly for God because we may not feel as much need for Him. Uncomfortable circumstances motivate us to seek and worship God more.

Read Proverbs 3:5-6 in the margin. How much of our hearts should trust God?

all our hearts

2. Trials can teach us to DEPEND ON OURSELVES LESS.

Trials reveal what's happening in our faith life and how often we try to live apart from God. In hard times we often realize just how much we need God.

Read Jeremiah 17:9 in the margin. What is the truth about our hearts apart from God?

deceitful + sick

3. Trials can teach us to BECOME MORE LIKE CHRIST.

Finally, trials can help us to become more like Christ. This is something that we cannot do on our own. You can want to be like Christ, but God's power is necessary to transform the selfish motives and directions of your heart.

[5]*Trust in the* LORD *with all your heart and lean not on your own understanding;* [6]*in all your ways submit to him, and he will make your paths straight.*
(Proverbs 3:5-6)

The heart is deceitful above all things, and desperately sick; who can understand it?
(Jeremiah 17:9 ESV)

This means that God has to remove what no longer serves a healthy or helpful purpose in our lives.

Read Romans 12:2 in the margin. What must we allow God to do in our lives?

> Be transformed by the renewing of our minds

What are some of the persistent spiritual battles or doubts about God that you've been fighting?

> Do I have faith that God will supply what I need?
> Sometimes I am so fearful of terrible things that could happen I ask God to spare me ... that I cannot handle them.

When I reflect on times of trial in my life, I realize that many of them have shined a light on fears about God's provision, my identity, or my character as a leader. God allowed circumstances to force me to uncomfortable corners where, ultimately, He brought me to a place of honesty about the gap between what I proclaimed to others about God and the fears in my own heart and mind—fears that got in the way of living out what I believed.

As this study continues, I'll share many stories about the different wilderness seasons that I've faced in life. You'll also learn about the wilderness season that I've been in while writing this study. My heart's desire is that I will continue to learn from my trials and allow God to use them to make me more and more like Jesus.

In addition to this week's Memory Verse, there are other verses that paint a powerful picture of what wilderness trials can do in our faith-life to bless us—now and in the future.

Read Romans 5:3-5 below, and underline the qualities that hard times produce in our lives.

[3] Not only so, but we also glory in our sufferings, because we know that suffering produces perseverance; [4] perseverance, character; and character, hope. [5] And hope does not put us to shame, because God's love has been poured out into our hearts through the Holy Spirit, who has been given to us.

(Romans 5:3-5)

Do not conform to the pattern of this world, but be transformed by the renewing of your mind. Then you will be able to test and approve what God's will is— his good, pleasing and perfect will.

(Romans 12:2)

As you reflect on the three ways that God can use trials in your life for good, do any of those lessons stand out today? If so, write about it briefly:

Trials sometimes bring me back to you Lord. Sometimes I forget you.

Let's close our lesson today with Jesus' words—words we can believe because He has already accomplished through His death and resurrection what He proclaimed. So, we can stand in confidence that whatever we're facing today won't beat us. We already have victory!

Write John 16:33 below, and circle the word indicating what Jesus promises us.

I have told you all this so that you may have peace in me. Here on Earth you will have many trials and sorrows. But take heart because I have overcome the world.

Jesus acknowledges that you're going to have hard times because our world is broken. Yet He wants you to have peace, a sense of calm, and an assurance that whatever you're facing today, you aren't facing it alone. You can have peace in Him and know that He is with you and for you. Most of all, Jesus' victory over every trial is *your* victory. You may not feel victorious today, but victory is yours when you put your hand in His and walk through your wilderness with Him.

Prayer

God, I am grateful that You never waste any of the good or bad experiences in my life. As I reflect on how You use my trials to help me see You clearer, depend on myself less, and learn to be more like Christ, I pray I always remember that You love, care for, and prepare me every step of the way. In Jesus' name. Amen.

Day 4: What's Tempting You?

There are some powerful comparisons and contrasts between how Jesus and the Israelites handled their wilderness experience. Both Jesus and the Israelites experienced dramatic God-moments before entering the stark unknown of the wilderness. As we've seen, the Israelites began complaining and talking about going back to Egypt while Jesus humbly submitted to the Holy Spirit's leading.

As we learn from this week's Memory Verse, challenges expose our faith-life. Yesterday we studied the first four wilderness trials, and our study today is devoted to the fifth trial: temptation.

Can you imagine having to deal face-to-face with Satan for one minute or even one second? Not only did Jesus encounter Satan; the tempter brought his A game. He wanted to trip Jesus up, no doubt hoping to derail Jesus' purpose for coming to earth, which was to seek and save the lost. Jesus knew that we'd face temptation. So, Jesus wanted to show us that the power of God living within us equips us to overcome our human desires, which can get out of control.

We all face temptation. I read an article about some research conducted by a well-known company related to the top five self-reported temptations in America.[7] According to the findings, they are the temptation to:

1. over-indulge in fear and worry,
2. procrastinate,
3. eat too much,
4. overuse electronics or social media, and
5. be lazy.

The article indicates that some temptations were reported at higher or lower rates depending on age or gender. But the author points out the bottom line of temptation, which gets at the heart of it all: "Most of the time temptation begins with something good: food, rest, God-approved sex, the need to be loved and accepted."[8]

It's not a sin to be tempted. Temptation comes in all shapes, forms, and sizes. However, the one thing we must remember is that temptation does not come from God (see James 1:3). Unfortunately, many of us have been shamed and silenced for feeling tempted. Jesus faced temptation, and He shows us the way to freedom when temptation tries to ensnare us.

Not many people love to sit around the dinner table and talk about the temptations they're facing. I'd venture to guess that you aren't excited about discussing what's wooing you away from loving God and others with the other women in your group. But we *need* to talk about temptation. It's real. It's powerful. And we all are dealing with temptation in one form or another.

Here's how I define temptation:

> **Temptation** – *An invitation that would distract or derail our pursuit of God.*

Today we're going to look at temptation. Jesus faced temptation in the wilderness because He knew that we'd face it in our lives.

5In your relationships with one another, have the same mindset as Christ Jesus:
6Who, being in very nature God, did not consider equality with God something to be used to his own advantage; 7rather, he made himself nothing by taking the very nature of a servant, being made in human likeness. (Philippians 2:5-7)

For we do not have a high priest who is unable to empathize with our weaknesses, but we have one who has been tempted, in every way, just as we are—yet he did not sin. (Hebrews 4:15)

Read Philippians 2:5-7 and Hebrews 4:15 in the margin. What do you learn about why it was necessary for Jesus to experience temptation?

He was a servant
He became human, ~~so~~ deliberately so!!

Here's what one scholar wrote about why God's Holy Spirit led Jesus into the wilderness: "Jesus was tempted so that every creature in heaven, on earth, and under the earth might know that Jesus Christ is the Conqueror."[9]

In difficult times, it's easy to think thoughts such as, *No one could possibly understand how I feel,* or *It's not fair that I have to go through this.* Maybe you don't know of anyone in your life who is facing similar circumstances as you, but Jesus understands. Not only does Jesus empathize with our weaknesses, but according to Hebrews 4:15, He also was tempted in every way, as we are; but he did not sin. Before Christ, the Israelites relied upon high priests to offer sacrifices to God on their behalf for the forgiveness of sin. However, the high priest couldn't make sacrifices for the people until he'd made an atoning sacrifice for his own sin (Hebrews 5:3). Jesus was and is the perfect high priest because He did not sin but sacrificed Himself for our sin.

It has been said that Jesus came to earth to show us what God was like. Jesus humbly took on our human bodies and limitations (Philippians 2:5-7) so that we could see how the power of God living within us can help us overcome temptation—keeping our human desires from getting out of control.

In the first book of the Bible, we see what happened when human desire met temptation. Our world has never been the same since.

Read Genesis 2:16-17. From what tree did God tell Adam not to eat? What would happen if he did?

Knowledge of good + evil
"You will surely die"

God's instructions were pretty straightforward. Since God had proclaimed that everything He created was very good, there were amazing options all around Adam. If I'd been in Adam's position, I would have eaten all the avocados my stomach could hold! God blessed Adam with abundance and gave him boundaries for his protection. Yet it wasn't enough.

To clarify, the Tree of the Knowledge of Good and Evil wasn't evil. There was nothing wrong with that tree. However, that tree was an invitation for Adam and Eve to trust God. God wanted Adam and Eve to trust that He had the knowledge of good and evil and they didn't need to know it.

Read Genesis 3:1. What question does the serpent ask Eve?

"did God really say you must not eat from the trees in the garden?"

Read Genesis 3:2-4 and answer the following:

How does Eve's response differ from God's instructions to Adam in Genesis 2:16-17?

How does the serpent contradict God's instructions? (v. 4)

He says we will be like God.

Much of our focus on temptation is external. We categorize people, things, or places as temptations. But the reality is that all forms of temptation begin when we question God's heart and whether or not He cares about our happiness and security.

Notice how Eve mixed and mashed up God's instructions. God told Adam not to eat from the tree. Eve embellished and added that God told them not to *touch* it. While the addition of another requirement is subtle, warping God's instructions often opens the door to warping our perception of God's heart.

Once our perception of God's love for us is warped, we fall prey to tempting enticements that promise to give us what we think God will not.

Read Genesis 3:5-6. How does the serpent contradict God's proclamation?

Said that you will be like God.

Verse 6 describes what happens next. What is the shift in Eve's mindset?

She wanted the wisdom eating the fruit could give you.

I shudder at these words in verse 6 (NLT): "The woman was convinced." What did Eve question about God's heart that sent her down the slippery slope of believing the serpent's lie? I must turn this question on myself. How many times have I been convinced that God didn't want what I really wanted, so I stretched my hands out, forcing or finding my own solutions?

It's not a sin to be tempted, so you don't have to beat yourself up for feeling the pull or pressure toward someone or something that is less than God's best for you. Here's a provocative question: what if your temptation is trying to expose you to areas where you're struggling to trust God's heart for you? Here are three insights about temptation that may depressurize or demagnetize temptation's effect on you so that you can break free and run back toward God's best for you and others.

Temptation Insight #1: Temptation starts with our minds, not our actions.

What's so hard about temptation for us? What are some of the lies we can believe about a temptation?

That we know better than God That we don't trust God so we take things in our own hands

The crazy thing is that the serpent never forced the fruit into Adam and Eve's hands but only suggested they eat it. When I think about the cookies that sit on my kitchen counter, I realize they aren't bothering anybody. The object of our temptation isn't our problem. Our trust issues toward God are the problem.

Temptation Insight #2: We're often tempted by what we think God won't give us another way.

Look at the top five temptations at the beginning of today's study (page 33). Do any of those temptations ever pop up in your life? If so, write about it briefly:

Of course I'm lazy I procrastinate I want too much!!

How often do our fears and worries about our relationships tempt us to fix or force solutions that either manipulate others or cheat us out of God's best for us? Adam and Eve grabbed on to their temptation and, in one bite, they wrecked their mortal souls.

As devastating as Adam and Eve's sin is, God reveals His compassionate heart toward His fallen creation—even though there would be consequences that would continue through all generations.

Read Genesis 3:16. What are the two punishments that God gives to Eve?

1. *childbirth will be painful*

2. *your husband will rule over you*

This leads us to our next temptation insight.

Temptation Insight #3: If you've felt a strong pull to fix or have things your own way, there's a spiritual root for that tendency.

What are some of the people, places, or things that you try to fix, force, or control?

Work — do I want good for them or for me?
My children
I want them to realize what is important to me
too much so

Okay, if you've gone through childbirth, you might be feeling a little salty toward Eve right now. Though we have the option of pain-numbing medicines to offset the pain of childbirth, if we want that option, unfortunately, there's no medication that keeps us from desiring to push for power over authority.

I don't know what you know about this second consequence, but it's something that I think about often. There's a desire inside me that I can't explain, but it's a little voice that often sounds like "I can fix this" or "I can fix *them*." Even if your tendency is not to control, we all struggle in one way or another with the desire for things to go our way.

Again, we all deal with temptation. For years I've battled the temptation to use comfort food as a soothing substitute instead of turning to God in times of sadness. Other times I've battled the temptation to pursue career success instead of finding my significance in God. While I love social media, I've had to battle the temptation to keep it from stealing my Bible study or prayer time with God.

Temptation is real. It can feel like a gravitational pull that sometimes we're not completely sure we want to fight. We can feel it, but we're not defenseless against it.

Read 1 Corinthians 10:13 in the margin. When you're tempted, what does God do for you?

He provides a way for me to endure

How has God provided a way out for you when you've been tempted?

One of the best defenses against temptation is to avoid it before it can tempt you. Is there something or someone in your life that tempts you away from God's best for you? What are some ways that you can put boundaries into your life to keep yourself far away from temptation?

[Work] —> boundries
—> ways to be kind

In Christian circles, whenever we talk about temptation, topics around sex and pornography usually pop up. However, there are related emotional temptations that need to be addressed as well.

For example, I worked on staff at my local church for many years; and early in my career, our founding senior pastor introduced a set of ten guidelines for staff interactions. In our context, men and women who were not married to each other were advised against sharing intimate marriage details with each other. I also chose to refrain from meeting one-on-one with a married man in a private space. While I wasn't concerned about getting involved in an inappropriate relationship, I wanted to protect myself from the trappings of temptation because it often occurs when we least expect it. Similar emotional temptations can occur in almost every area of our lives.

Read James 5:16 in the margin. What happens when you talk about your struggles?

allows others to pray for you

The truth of this verse is so powerful because confession actually brings healing. We can be confident that when we confess our sins, God will forgive us (1 John 1:9), but it is in sharing our sins and struggles with one another that we find healing. I am so grateful for my Christian counselors, Bible study groups, spiritual sisters, and accountability partner. With so many people in my life to share my struggles with, I have experienced healing in so many ways! The inverse is also true: when we hide our problems, we end up bringing more pain into our lives. Over the years I've found that one of the best ways to get to the heart of the matter and short-circuit the pull of temptation is to talk with a trusted Christian friend.

Is there a truth or a verse from our study today that is resonating strongly in your heart right now? If so, write it below.

Is there a situation or area where you aren't sure that God will do what's best for you? Is there someone or something that promises to "fill in" where you are worried that God will let you down?

I don't know what you're dealing with today, but if you are facing temptation on a big or small scale, there's hope! Whether you are tempted to reply to those flirty texts from the attractive married person in your office, are binge eating, or are not reporting the undeserved extra money in your retirement check, today is the last day that you need to allow temptation to draw you farther away from God's best in your life. Pray today and ask God for help! Remember the promise found in 1 Corinthians 10:13, because God will provide a way out for you.

Prayer

Dear God, thank You for Your heart of love and good plans for me. As I reflect on the temptations in my life, help me to turn my eyes away from those temptations and choose to trust Your love and heart toward me. During tough times, it's hard to keep that perspective, but I choose to believe this today. In Jesus' name. Amen.

Day 5: Will You Give In, Give Up, or Let Go?

Years ago I participated in an arm wrestling contest. Not because I had a dream of being a professional arm wrestler or anything like that. In fact, it was Children's Day in Honduras, and the church hosting our missions team planned a fun day of family activities, including "mom arm wrestling."

I sat down opposite my Honduran friend, Patti. Her then-teenaged daughter stood cheering in the background. My daughters were back in the US, so a few of the Honduran kids pretended that I was their mom and cheered for me.

Patti and I propped our elbows on the white folding table and giggled while clasping hands. The last time that I arm wrestled was...never. But dozens of kids, missions team members, and others stood around us, waiting for the referee to start the match.

I threw all of my energy into that one arm. So did Patti! Our forearms quivered, but there was no significant movement in one direction or the other. This went on for about a minute, and I started to feel really tired. I liked Patti. We shouldn't have been arm wrestling each other; we should have been off somewhere sharing a slice of cake. Someone captured a picture of my wrestling match with Patti about a minute into our match. The wide-eyed look on my face could have been translated, "I can't keep holding this; I sure hope it's over soon!"

Does my arm wrestling match remind you of any situation you're in right now? Are you trying to wrestle a situation at home, at work, or in a relationship that you can't seem to fix? When we face problems but we're unable to protect, fix, or get something back on track, it's easy for us to feel overwhelmed or discouraged.

Today we're going to go backward in the story of the Israelites and learn some insights from what happened when God first called Moses to lead them out of slavery into the wilderness. Moses didn't have the confidence that he could do what God called him to do, but God spoke assurances and promises that can uplift and encourage our hearts, as well. Whatever you're facing today isn't on your shoulders to solve. As Moses discovered, God's power is all you need!

Read Exodus 3:1-2. Where was Moses when he saw the blazing bush?

Wilderness. - Mt Sinai

Before he led the Israelites, Moses spent forty years in the wilderness as a shepherd. It's interesting that God chose him to be their leader since Moses would have been familiar with the wilderness living conditions.

Moses sees the burning bush that does not burn up, and so he approaches it. Then he hears God speaking to him.

Read Exodus 1:7-8, and complete the following statements:

God tells Moses that He has heard the Israelites'

cries of distress . (v. 7)

God says that He will _____ *rescue* _____ the Israelites
from the Egyptians. (v. 8)

God plans to bring the people of Israel to a land flowing with
_____ *milk* _____ and _____ *honey* _____. (v. 9)

As you read earlier this week, the Egyptians enslaved the Israelites and treated them horribly. The Israelites were trapped in a situation in which they had no control, and God heard their cries for help. God not only laid out a plan to rescue the Israelites, but He promised to resettle the people in a place where the phrase "flowing with milk and honey" would be a symbol of God's generosity.[10]

When God spoke to Moses, the people of Israel were still suffering and in slavery, yet God declared His promises over their lives. This is important to us because whenever we're in a wilderness season marked by any one of the trials that we studied earlier this week, God promises to do what He says He will do, even though we have to trust His timing. We can trust God to keep His promises because He cannot lie (see Hebrews 10:23). However, it's important to remember that not all of God's promises will be fulfilled in our time here on earth.

Look up these promises from God and summarize each one:

Deuteronomy 31:8

do not be afraid or discouraged the Lord will take care ahead of you ooche will not abandon you!

Psalm 34:17

The Lord hears his people when they call to him for help, He rescues them from their troubles

Isaiah 43:2

★ *God will be c̄ you when things are hard*

John 8:36

Jesus sets you free from your sin

Revelation 21:4

He will wipe every tear from their eyes and there will be no more death or sorrow or crying or pain. All these things are gone forever

Which one or more of these promises do you need today? Why?

He is always c̄ me + the promise of tomorrow

There are thousands of promises made by God in the Bible. The reason I chose to highlight these promises is because wilderness seasons can make us forget God's faithfulness, and we need to remember that God has a future for us.

When the Israelites were in slavery and unable to change or control their circumstances, they cried out to God for help and held on to the hope that He would show up in their circumstances. Eventually, He did! God called Moses. However, Moses struggled with the role that God called him to play.

Read Exodus 3:11-15. What are Moses' objections to God's instructions?

What holy name does God tell Moses to give the people when they ask who sent him?

Yahweh

Moses protested because he didn't feel qualified to lead, represent God, or communicate well. Yet the success of God's plan didn't rely on Moses' capacity or capabilities. God didn't ask Moses to do anything other than show up in the places where God sent him and share the message that God gave him to share. God proclaimed that it would be His power that would do the work to free the Israelite people.

Read Exodus 3:19-21. God tells Moses that the king of Egypt won't let the Israelites go unless what happens?

a mighty hand forces him

As a bonus, what will God cause the Egyptians to give the Israelites as they leave? (v. 21)

gifts

In verse 19, God explains that nothing can free the Israelites from slavery unless a mighty hand forces the king of Egypt to let them go. It would not be Moses who would force the king to free God's people; it would be God doing the work. Even as Moses questioned his ability to show up and do a good job, God wasn't worried. As one writer describes it, "When we tell God our weaknesses, we aren't sharing anything He doesn't already know. The will of God will never lead you where the power of God can't enable you, so walk by faith in His promises."[11]

Is there a situation you've been trying to fix but nothing has worked?
If so, describe it briefly:

Clare

So many other things I tried to "fix" but God ultimately it was

How has the constant stress of the situation impacted your life?

your work + hard. Thank you!!

During trials and wilderness seasons, we often spend a lot of mental energy trying to stay in whatever fight is most important to us—the fight for financial security, our marriage, our child's survival, our jobs, or our faith. However, fighting in a situation that you can't change, control, or conquer will wear you down and eventually wear you out. At a certain point, we'll choose one of three responses. Here are the first two:

1. Giving up is losing hope.
2. Giving in is caving in to another's agenda.

Are there any places in your heart or mind where you feel like giving up or giving in?

Perhaps you're at the point where you've given up or are considering it. You're exhausted from trying to push all of the buttons, pull all of the levers, and fix all of the problems. Maybe you've given in to the unhealthy requests and demands of others because you're afraid or you don't know what else to do. Like Moses, you've got lots of excuses even though you know what God is calling you to do.

But hold on. There's a third option that can lift the weight of problems from your heart and position you to experience God's power working in and through your life. That option is not giving up or giving in but, rather, letting go.

3. Letting go is not trying to fix or force a solution but living in faith that God will do what is best.

Another word for letting go is *surrender*. Letting go, or surrendering, is a prayer, a plan, and a process. There are some situations where we'll be able to let go more easily than others. There also are times when we realize that we can let go in the moment, but then we move back into trying to control when we don't feel that God is moving fast enough. Over time, as we practice letting go and living like Jesus, we discover what it looks and feels like to completely surrender others and outcomes to God, leaving them totally in His hands.

Here's a visual of what I think the letting go process looks like. Again, it's not a step-by-step process but rather an ongoing process of asking questions that can help us move away from being a remote control for others or outcomes and move toward learning how to open our hands to invite God into whatever we're facing.

Here are the questions that you can ask in the Letting Go Loop:

Awareness—Am I trying to control others or outcomes right now?

Arrest—What do I need to stop trying to protect, fix, or force to make happen?

Acceptance—Where do I need to acknowledge the reality that I do not have control but God can and will handle it?

FaithFULL Action—How can I show faith, unconditional love, and wisdom without control-loving behaviors?

You might not feel like you can let go yet, and that's okay. We're going to spend the coming weeks together learning how to let go and live like Jesus. But I want to share two important verses that encourage me when my control-loving whispers seem too loud to ignore and I get so discouraged or frustrated that I want to give up.

Read 2 Corinthians 10:4 in the margin. According to this verse, what weapons do you have available to you to help you fight back against control-loving mindsets and behaviors?

[4]We use God's mighty weapons, not worldly weapons, to knock down the strongholds of human reasoning and to destroy false arguments.
(2 Corinthians 10:4 NLT)

Now read Galatians 6:9 in the margin. Why does Paul encourage us to keep going and not give up trusting God?

So let's not get tired of doing what is good. At just the right time we will reap a harvest of blessing if we don't give up.
(Galatians 6:9 NLT)

The word *good* in Galatians 6:9 is the Greek word *kalos*, meaning "an outward sign of the inward good, noble, honorable character."[12] This means that while we may face circumstances and outcomes beyond our control, we don't have to give up on making the daily decisions that reflect our trust in God.

Moses gives God a lot of excuses as to why he isn't the right person for the job. He wants to give up before he ever gets started. However, he *does* follow God's call in obedience, and he has faith that God will fulfill His promises—even though he protests a lot and doesn't feel very confident.

On the first day of this week's study, I shared a story about being facedown on my kitchen floor. On that day, I felt like giving up on my faith because that season of testing had pushed me to the limits. Even though I'd grown up in the church and, at the time, worked part-time for my church, I was ready to throw in the towel. I never thought there would be a day when I'd be tempted to walk away from my faith, but I was so disappointed with God and disgusted with myself that I'd lost hope life could be better.

As I sat up and leaned my back against the lower cupboards, I thought about what my life would be like if God was no longer a part of it. It didn't take long for me to realize that I would be on my own. As I considered that I needed God because I couldn't handle my unmanageable life on my own, I was challenged in that moment to stop trying to manage my life and allow God to do His job.

At that point, nothing had changed but God used that desperate difficult moment to begin transforming my beliefs. It was at that point when I decided that I would stop trying to do God's job for him. From my kitchen floor I declared the following: *God, if it's gonna get done, you're going to have to do it!*

Now, it's your turn. Are you ready to make a declaration in your life? Here are a few questions for you:

- Are you tired of trying to fix problems that aren't in your control?
- Are you tired of trying to help people who don't want to do what's healthy or helpful for themselves?
- Are you tired of playing God?

Each week I will be introducing a Surrender Principle, which is a short saying that you can repeat to yourself in moments when you're tempted to pull out one of those SHINE control-loving behaviors in order to get what you want. Here's our first one:

SURRENDER PRINCIPLE #1:

I am not in control of others or outcomes.

You know that this is true, but sometimes, it's helpful to have a short sentence to repeat as a reminder. Now, I'm going to invite you to take a tangible first step toward letting go and making a declaration of surrender to God. You can do this by filling in the blanks below:

My Declaration of Surrender

Dear God, I am tired of trying to fix/solve

_____.

In the past I have tried to _____

_____,

and I have felt discouraged and defeated because this situation is out of my control.

But God, You can handle this situation. So today I surrender myself and my situation to You. Over the next few weeks of this study, I commit to learning what it means to walk in surrender. But for today, I declare that I am willing to let go of this situation and give it to You.

I surrender.

Signed: _____

Date: _____

Prayer

Thank You, God, for being God. There are situations in my life that I cannot handle, and I am grateful that You can. So, as I've written in my declaration, I'm giving those situations over to You. Thank You for taking care of me and what I cannot control. In Jesus' name. Amen.

Week 1 Video Viewer Guide

scorekeeping

S ~~tonewalling~~ - being silent

H elicopter (micromanaging/overprotecting)

I nterrupting

N agging

E xcessive planning _____ or Overstocking

Remember God's ♥ for you

A: (You are) ____always____ loved.

Psalm 52:8

B: ____Believe____ that God is for you.

God is out to give wilderness place of emotional + spiritual confusion to you

Exodus 3:7-8

Exodus 16:1-4

God takes care of His children at ____all____ times,
especially ____hard____ times.

Matthew 6:11 - give us today our daily bread

Matthew 6:34

Joshua 1:9

Therefore do not worry about tomorrow, for tomorrow will worry about itself. Each day has enough trouble of its own

c: Challenge _____ yourself to trust God and let go.

Surrender Principle #1

I am not in control of ____others____ or ____outcomes____.

strength comes from God

LETTING GO!!

LIVE like Jesus!!

S scorekeeping

H - helicopter

I - interrupting putting our hands in someone elses business

N - nagging

rare place of opportunity

Not in absence of wisdom

Careful + truthful = living or not careless living

Week 2

What Are You Hungry For?

(Matthew 4:2)

Memory Verse

But seek first his kingdom and his righteousness, and all these things will be given to you as well.
(Matthew 6:33)

Letting go can be a challenge for any woman who struggles with control-loving tendencies. As a woman who battles the deep desire to protect, fix, and direct the people or problems in my life, I am a fellow traveler with you on this journey to let go and learn to live more like Jesus.

At the end of last week's study, you had an opportunity to sign "My Declaration of Surrender." Whether or not you are ready to take that first step, I trust that you will when you're ready. Letting go of control-loving behaviors and learning how to deal with the desire to control are not easy tasks, so don't beat yourself up if this is your struggle. I encourage you to pray and ask God to help you truly embrace even just the first step of not being in control of others or outcomes. To help you take an intentional step toward surrender, I'm including a Daily Surrender Prayer at the beginning of each lesson for the remainder of our study.

Whether you've taken the first step toward surrender by signing the declaration, you're still considering it, or you're a veteran in the surrendered camp, all of us battle what I like to call a challenging case of the "I wants." This strong feeling captures your desire for a person, place, feeling, or thing, and you can't get it off your mind until you get it. The "I wants" are powerful feelings that we can't always put into words and, if left unmanaged, might cause us to follow those feelings and cause pain or harm to ourselves and others. Just because we love Jesus doesn't mean we don't have to deal with the "I wants"—and that includes me too.

I remember the time this well-intentioned, Jesus-loving girl lost control and ate an entire pecan pie because I couldn't stop myself. God used that embarrassing out-of-control moment to reveal that my "I wants" were only a symptom of deeper hungers that rumbled within. While hunger is a physical condition, it also can describe an intense emotional need. The "I wants" pop up whenever I'm hungry for something deeper such as love, belonging, satisfaction, or purpose. Furthermore, I've learned that just because I let go of trying to control what I want doesn't mean I lose the desire for it. So the question is, *How do we deal with our desires or the "I wants" in situations where we don't have control?* If we don't figure out how to redirect those hungers, we'll find ourselves sliding back into control-loving behaviors of fleeing, forcing, or fixing.

In this week's study, Jesus faces the first of three temptations from Satan. This temptation strikes hard at us as human beings because it's the temptation to believe that we can use God to give us what we want. However, Jesus teaches us that the invitation in the midst of this temptation is to discover that God is and will always be 100 percent what we need.

Day 1: "I Want..."

Daily Surrender Prayer:

God, I choose to surrender my anxiety *to You today.*

Do you remember the good ole days when Black Friday shopping meant waking up at four or five a.m. the day after Thanksgiving to stand in line at an electronics or big-box store in order to get that big ticket item you'd been dreaming about snagging at a great price? I really admired the dedicated bargain hunters who pitched tents and snacked on leftover turkey the night before because I live in the Midwest where late November means cold, if not snowy, weather.

While there's an important debate about whether or not online shopping helps or hurts local economies, the competitive Black Friday shopping that resulted in injuries, fights, and even deaths illuminates a deeper spiritual issue. One Black Friday I watched two people slug it out over a three-dollar waffle maker. That chaotic scene prompted me to ask myself, *What's really going on here?*

Sometimes our "I wants" cost more than just the price tag. There are some things we desire that end up costing us dearly in our physical, relational, financial, or spiritual lives. Perhaps you know someone who wanted a house so badly that she signed a mortgage that left finances teetering on the edge. Maybe you know a friend who hungered for love or acceptance, and that deep hunger may have led her to say yes to friendships or relationships that ended up hurting her in the long run.

Today we explore Jesus' time in the wilderness before He is first tempted. Jesus chooses to endure his wilderness experience as wholly human, and in doing so, teaches us how to approach our deepest hungers and how to surrender those hungers to the only One who satisfies. As we read, I invite you to think about where you're struggling with a hard case of the "I wants" and challenge yourself to answer the question, *What's really going on here?*

Read Matthew 4:2. How long did Jesus fast?

40 days

What was Jesus' physical condition after fasting for that period of time?

hungry + weak

While fully divine, Jesus experienced the wilderness as a human. We know this because Jesus became hungry, a human experience. Forty days is a long time to go without food, so it's no surprise that He was hungry.

Why did Jesus spend forty days fasting? Let's look at two important reasons that not only tie Jesus' experience to the past but also show how Jesus demonstrates His love and desire to connect with us at the place of our deepest hunger and need.

Extra Insight

"Forty days is about the longest a human can fast without permanent bodily harm."[1]

1. Jesus' forty-day fast mirrors Moses' forty-day experience with God.

Jesus' forty days in the wilderness mirror Moses' forty days with God on Mount Sinai as the Israelites began their journey into the wilderness.

Read Exodus 34:28. What did Moses *not* do while he was with God for forty days?

fasted

During this time, God gave Moses instructions on how the people were to live and teachings on His character and holiness, as well as the promises that God would fulfill for His people.

Moses makes a request of God knowing very little about the journey that lies ahead. We can make this same request of God each day that we face days in the wilderness as well.

Read Exodus 34:9. What request does Moses make of God?

travel c̄ us, forgive us our sins, claim us as your own possession

2. Jesus fasted forty days so that he could identify with deep human weakness.

As a human, Jesus fasts from nourishment in the wilderness. We're not told whether this was by the Spirit's leading or initiated by Christ. However, the act of fasting for such a long period of time would have weakened Jesus' physical body to the most vulnerable state possible, but He did this to fully identify with the depths of our human experience so that He could lead us to freedom.

Read Hebrews 2:14-18 and answer the questions that follow.

14Since the children have flesh and blood, he too shared in their humanity so that by his death he might break the power of him who holds the power of death—that is, the devil— ¹⁵and free those who all their lives were held in slavery by their fear of death. ¹⁶For surely it is not angels he helps, but Abraham's descendants. ¹⁷For this reason he had to be made like them, fully human in every way, in order that he might become a merciful and faithful high priest in service to God, and that he might make atonement for the sins of the people. ¹⁸Because he himself suffered when he was tempted, he is able to help those who are being tempted.

(Hebrews 2:14-18)

Underline "break the power" in verse 14.

Circle the word *free* in verse 15.

Why did Jesus have to come in a human body? (v. 17)

to make atonement for all people

Jesus wasn't just tempted; He also ___*suffered*___ when He was tempted (v. 18)

Ultimately, what was the purpose of Jesus enduring suffering and temptation? (v. 18)

To help those who are being tempted

Jesus suffered during His time of temptation. He wasn't skipping around the wilderness just running down the clock until He could go home. What Jesus went through was hard, just as whatever you're going through today may be hard. Whenever we're going through a hard time, we may not connect with the person who tells us to "buck up" or "cheer up," but we are drawn to the person who says "me too."

Read John 2:25. What does this verse say about Jesus' knowledge of our human needs and struggles?

He already knew

What are the "I wants" in your life right now?

things, power, position respect from people

You don't have to feel condemned, embarrassed, or ashamed of your "I wants," whether it's desperation to have a clean house, to have a relationship, or even to see someone you love experience the saving love and grace of Jesus. It's how you act on your "I wants" that God is concerned with. While it's a good thing to want someone you love to know Jesus, tricking him or her to go to church isn't the way to go about it. This is where that letting-go loop comes in to help you back off of those SHINE control-loving behaviors and let go and let God.

Extra Insight

"Christ has put on our feelings along with our flesh."[2]
–John Calvin

Memory Verse Reflection

*) also "crave" ✓

Write Matthew 6:33 below. Circle the word *seek*.

But (seek) first his kingdom + his righteousness, and all these things will be given to you as well

The word *seek* is *zeteo* in Greek. Among the various definitions of the word is "crave," meaning to have a strong tasting desire for something. *C*rave is more than just hoping that it works out. In this verse, crave is over-focus on desiring this more than anything else.

According to Matthew 6:33, what are we to seek (or crave) as followers of Christ?

his kingdom + righteousness

Jesus speaks this wisdom just after teaching the crowd about how God takes care of their physical needs. I'd like to think that the women in the audience were especially tuned in as Jesus said, "So do not worry, saying, 'What shall we eat?' or 'What shall we drink?' or 'What shall we wear?'" (Matthew 6:31). He knows us so well, right?

As Jesus calls His believers to seek the kingdom of God, we're to elevate God's priorities before and above our own. This isn't easy to do. If it was, then Jesus wouldn't have needed to teach about it.

Is there a situation in your life that you're prioritizing over your relationship with God?

staff
pride ooo my home

What is Jesus' promise to us when we live God's priorities before our own interests?

" all these things will be given to you as well

As you conclude today's study, I pray that you feel comforted and encouraged by the beautiful truth that Jesus sees your struggle through the perspective of "me, too" rather than criticism or condemnation. Never forget that God is for you and your part is to keep your eyes on Him.

Prayer

Dear God, You know that I am hungry for help/hope/healing related to _____ _____ *in my life. It's so hard to have such a longing inside. Sometimes it feels like it's the only thing that I can think about. However, God, I want to crave You like Jesus teaches in Matthew 6:33. I give You permission to work in my heart to help me see Your love, Your glory, and Your power in increasing measure. In Jesus' name. Amen.*

Day 2: Only Jesus Satisfies

Daily Surrender Prayer:

God, I choose to surrender

~~wine~~

_____

_____

to You today.

My favorite candy bar is Snickers. I've loved the combination of peanuts, caramel, and chocolate since I was old enough to beg my grandfather for the money and permission to ride my bike across town to the candy store to buy one. Some time ago, the company began decorating the backs of their chocolate bars with the phrase "Snickers Satisfies."

As a busy working woman, Snickers filled the empty space of the "I wants" in my life that I wasn't getting. If I wanted peace but couldn't get it, Snickers could calm me down. If wanted to feel a little energy boost but didn't have time to take a break, Snickers would give me a shot of sugar. If I wanted to treat myself but didn't have time for a massage or manicure, I could open up a Snickers bar in my car and enjoy that treat.

Snickers did satisfy. But not for long. One day I was at the store to buy yet another Snickers bar when I finally asked the question, *Why did I expect that little chocolate to fill this big hunger rumbling inside of me?* I was eating more and more little candy bars each day, but I was still stressed, dragging, and feeling like I was taking care of everyone else but me.

What have you been doing to satisfy your case of the "I wants"?

Wine, chocolate
rich food

In Matthew 4, the devil proposes an opportunity for Jesus to satisfy his physical hunger after fasting for forty days and forty nights. However, Jesus' response gives us the path to lasting satisfaction that nothing on earth can provide.

Read Matthew 4:2-4 (NIV) and fill in the blanks below and following.

1. The devil came to Jesus and began by saying "If you are the ___Son and God___..." (v. 3) tell these stones to become bread

First, we notice in verse 3 that the devil came to Jesus. (It occurs to me that it's not a question of will Satan come; we must anticipate and prepare for the eventuality that he will come.) Satan begins by tempting Jesus to use His divine nature to satisfy His human desires. After all, Jesus had been in the wilderness with no comforts or ease. I can almost hear Satan whisper, "You say that you're God and if that's that the case, then snap your fingers and make your little hunger problem go away."

However, Jesus declared before he was baptized that he did so to fulfill all righteousness (Matthew 3:15), so his divine nature was always to be used to please God and not to indulge human desires. Satan's goal is to twist our human desires for good things into destructive behaviors that can destroy us. As Jesus said, "The thief comes only to steal and kill and destroy; I have come that they may have life, and have it to the full" (John 10:10).

2. The devil tempts Jesus to turn the stones into loaves of ___bread___. (v. 3)

I don't know about you, but if I'd fasted for forty days and forty nights while isolated and alone, just about anything would look good to eat. Satan tempts Jesus to turn the stones into loaves of bread.

Satan's first temptation targets Jesus' deepest point of physical weakness: hunger. This reminds me that Satan is going to put pressure on my greatest human need that feels the weakest in the moment. So, wherever you're feeling the most unfulfilled or empty, you're likely to be tempted to satisfy that space.

For me, emotional eating is a temptation. In the space between what I've surrendered and the hunger for it, there's a temptation to fill that empty space with brownies, cookies, or anything sweet and creamy. I've battled this temptation for decades. Praise God that He has led me toward surrender as well as some specific spiritual disciplines that allow me to experience victory and freedom, even though I still have to fight the battle.

While Scripture doesn't give many other details, I have no problem imagining this scene. I can see Satan holding a platter of lightly toasted, rounded loaves shaped just like the rocks surrounding Jesus on the ground. In my mind

Extra Insight

Satan, another name for the devil used by Jesus (Matthew 4:10), means "adversary, one who opposes the law."[4]

each loaf sports a glossy, shiny, buttery top with pools of melted butter around the bread and dripping off the sides.

3. Jesus' response to Satan: "It is written, *people* shall not live on *bread* alone, but on *every word* that comes from the mouth of *God*." (v. 4)

Notice that Jesus' reply begins with "It is written," showing that He was deferring to God's Holy Word rather than voicing his own opinion or rebuttal. Notice how Jesus doesn't argue with Satan; rather, His first move is to elevate the authority of God's words.

Additionally, Jesus doesn't bargain with Satan—or even Himself. Since we know that Jesus was tempted, He may have considered turning a stone or two into bread.

For we do not have a high priest who is unable to empathize with our weaknesses, but we have one who has been tempted in every way, just as we are—yet he did not sin.

(Hebrews 4:15)

Read Hebrews 4:15 in the margin. Jesus faced temptation, but how did He handle it?

Again, it's not a sin to be tempted. Jesus faced every kind of temptation that we face, and it was not sinful for Him to be tempted. This might provide some freedom from the whisper of condemnation, guilt, or shame if you've been beating yourself up over feeling a pull toward emotional eating, a desire to spend more than you can afford when shopping, an attraction toward someone who isn't God's best for you or some other temptation.

However, we must be on guard against compromise or putting ourselves in a situation where we're toying with the temptation. It's too easy for us to fall!

Is there an area of temptation where you're trying to figure out how to get a little bit of what you want without actually sinning? If so, write about it briefly:

The temptation of vanity and spending too much worried about my looks

Since emotional eating has been an issue in my life, during a time of tremendous stress of dealing with our family crisis, a career change, and the sudden loss of loved ones, I had to make the extreme decision to not keep desserts or sweets in my home. There's nothing sinful about having desserts or sweets, but for me the temptation to turn to them instead of turning to God is a battle that I can choose not to fight in this difficult season of life.

> How might you resist a specific temptation that might lead to sin by choosing some action—such as to delete something, to no longer buy something, to break up with someone, or to no longer walk/drive past somewhere?

While Satan entices Jesus to use his divine nature to pacify his human desire, Jesus didn't pull the God-card. By using the word *man*, Jesus communicates that He is facing temptation in humanity's shoes and models for us the way forward through temptation.

It's interesting to note that "Jesus responds to each temptation by quoting from Deuteronomy."[6] Here, in responding to the first temptation, Jesus quotes Deuteronomy 8:3. After the Israelites had spent their forty years in the wilderness, Moses taught a series of messages from God to prepare the people to finally enter the Promised Land. Jesus' response references what Moses taught the people as he asked them to reflect on their years of wandering.

> Read Deuteronomy 8:3 in the margin. Circle the portion of the verse that is similar to Jesus' reply to Satan.

> What does it mean to live by every word that comes from the mouth of the Lord?

To look to God for my everyday needs

Remember that God didn't provide manna to the children of Israel until they'd been on their own for over a month in the wilderness (see Exodus 16:1, 6-7). He let them get good and hungry so that they would realize that they couldn't take care of themselves on their own. However, it wasn't just their physical hunger that needed to be addressed but also their spiritual hunger. The Israelites needed God's guidance in the wilderness, but as we'll discover, they often rejected God's guidance in favor of following their own way.

We live by every word that comes from God when we are obedient to what God is calling us to do and how God is calling us to live. However, we're not convinced of our need to be obedient until we run into a few painful experiences that reinforce that we're not in control of people or outcomes.

He humbled you, causing you to hunger and then feeding you with manna, which neither you nor your ancestors had known, to teach you that man does not live on bread alone but on every word that comes from the mouth of the LORD.
(Deuteronomy 8:3)

For the word of
God is alive and
active. Sharper than
any double-edged
sword, it penetrates
even to dividing soul
and spirit, joints and
marrow; it judges
the thoughts and
attitudes of the heart.
(Hebrews 4:12)

Read Hebrews 4:12 in the margin. How deep can God's Word penetrate our lives?

Why do we need the truth of God's Word to cut so deep into our hearts, minds, and souls?

To keep me on track to ensure I live by God's word not my ? + desires

In the wilderness, Moses had an assistant named Joshua, who would eventually become the leader of the Israelites after Moses' death. Right before the Israelites entered the Promised Land, God spoke to Joshua and gave him important instructions on how to be successful in the Promised Land, even though Joshua had no idea or control over what was going to happen next. The following verse provides a powerful template for how we can learn to live by every word that comes from God.

Read Joshua 1:8 (NIV) and fill in the blanks below.

1. _____Study_____ this Book of the Law always on your lips;

2. _____Meditate_____ on it day and night, so that you may be careful...

3. to _____Obey_____ [obey] everything written in it.

4. Then you will be _____prosperous_____ and _____succeed in all you day_____

*Whose delight is in
the law of the LORD,
and who
meditates on his
law day and night.
(Psalm 1:2)*

It's here that God offers the footprints of how we walk in His way in order to experience true life, no matter what comes our way. While obedience is the end goal, we can't be obedient until we know and believe that what God says is true and best for us.

There is a real blessing when we take God's Word to heart and follow it. God's words in Joshua 1:8 are echoed elsewhere in Scripture.

Read Psalm 1:2 and Revelation 1:3 in the margin. What do these verses encourage us to do?

*Blessed is the
one who reads
aloud the words
of this prophecy,
and blessed are those
who hear it and
take to heart what is
written in it, because
the time is near.
(Revelation 1:3)*

How has God's wisdom in the Bible been a blessing in your life?

This current wilderness season of my life has included overwhelming emotional pain and all kinds of relational loss. However, most days I fall to my knees each morning to give thanks to God for the wisdom and truth of the Bible that literally gives me life. It's God's wisdom that has taught me to forgive instead of ruining my heart, mind, and soul in bitterness. God's truth has lit a path for me toward hope and purpose so that I have not followed my own path to self-centered or destructive behaviors. Within the pages of the Bible, I read stories of restoration and redemption, knowing that those stories were written long ago (Romans 15:4) to bring me hope while I wait for God to act in my circumstances.

You might be holding out for that person, place, or thing that you really want, but today I hope you can see that following God's path for your life will lead you to the only One you'll ever need.

Prayer

Dear God, I am so grateful that Jesus showed us the path to real life in the wilderness and that life is found only in following You. As I deal with the "I wants" in my life, what I desire is to want You more than anything else. In Jesus' name. Amen.

Day 3: Letting Go of the "I Wants"

What's the best meal you've ever had? Can you remember it? There's a particular meal that I enjoy from a small chain of Cajun-inspired seafood restaurants spread around the country. I can't tell you why this is my favorite meal on the planet. It just is!

For those who are curious, it's a platter featuring a lightly crusted tilapia topped with lump crab and covered with *beurre blanc* sauce, or as I like to call it, fancy butter. It comes with a side of steamed *haricot verts* (aka, green beans) and a buttery mound of spaghetti squash. This meal may not get you excited, but it's the kind of meal that tempts me to lick my plate right there in the restaurant. There's always more food on my plate than I can possibly eat, but that never stops me from trying. On more than one occasion, I've exclaimed, "I can't eat another bite!" However, at some point, either the next day or shortly thereafter, there will be a moment at which I will think, "Hmmm, I'm hungry," and head off looking for something to eat.

Daily Surrender Prayer:

God, I choose to surrender

_____

_____

_____

to You today.

All of us experience the "I wants," and sometimes we'll even use control-loving behaviors to get what we want. However, as much as we think that certain people, places, or things in our lives will satisfy us, the reality is that they don't, they won't, and more important, they can't. The tragedy is for us to think that they will.

Today we observe the Israelites in the wilderness and see what happens when God gives them exactly what they want. At the core of their "I wants" rumbled a dissatisfaction and distrust of God. They believed that if they got what they really wanted, then they would be happy. So God gives it to them in a dramatic way.

Read Numbers 11:1, 4-6, and answer the following:

What were the Israelites complaining about? (v. 1)

their hardship

What did the Israelites wish that they had? (v. 4)

meat, cucumbers, melons etc

The people claimed to have lost their _____.
(v. 6) *appetites*

The Israelites were discouraged. After camping in one area for almost a year, the wilderness was wearing on them. They were angry with the same God who had rescued them from slavery in Egypt and the same God who had miraculously provided manna in the wilderness so that they wouldn't have to watch their children starve to death.

The English Standard Version Bible records verse 4 as saying: "Now the rabble that was among them had a strong craving." The rabble were a group of non-Israelites who had fled from Egypt with the Israelites and who began to complain. Their attitude affected the Israelites, dusting up whatever seeds of discontent were in the Israelites' hearts, and soon the Israelites were complaining too. Apparently it didn't take long for the Israelites to forget the oppression of slavery and the harsh treatment they had faced in Egypt. Once the Israelites' hunger was in charge, they seemed to forget a lot of other important details.

The impact of the nonbelieving foreigners reminds me of the ancient wisdom that says, "Bad company corrupts good character" (1 Corinthians 15:33).

Are there nonbelievers in your life whose unbelief or distrust of God affects your attitude or faith negatively or encourages control-loving behaviors? If so, what are doubts they've planted, or discouragement they've spoken, that has caused you to doubt God's faithfulness or provision?

It's not clear why the non-Israelite travelers left Egypt to travel into the wilderness, but their attitude wasn't helping anyone. Perhaps you've got unbelieving friends or family who are watching your struggle; and since they don't understand spiritual matters, they might question why you're attempting to trust God.

Years ago, I remember talking with one woman whose husband had left their marriage after the loss of a child. She told me that her non-Christian girlfriends took her out one night and encouraged her to find a new man and not to worry if he was already married. She wisely rejected that suggestion, but she was tempted, especially since she was lonely and devastated over the loss of her child and her husband's unfaithfulness. When we're hurting or uncomfortable, we're more vulnerable to temptation as well as finding fault with God's provision in our lives.

In the verses that follow, the Israelites began complaining again, so Moses goes to God and basically says, "God, I can't take all of this complaining. If you love me, kill me now." Moses is deeply discouraged and for good reason.

In His great wisdom, God leverages the entire situation to not only revamp Moses' leadership structure to give him some relief (Numbers 11:16-17) but also to teach the Israelites a lesson about an ungodly hunger they'd let get out of control.

Read Numbers 11:18-23, and answer the following questions:

What did God tell Moses to share with the people about what was coming?

meat

God said He would send enough meat to last how long? (v. 19)

a month

What effect did God say that the meat would have on the people?

until you gag

Extra Insight

"In Israel, the quail is a migrating bird that arrives in droves along the shores of the Mediterranean Sea. Sometimes they are so tired after their migration that they can be caught by hand."[8]

Remember that old saying, "Be careful what you wish for because you just might get it"? God tells Moses to prepare the people because God is about to send them more meat than they could ever dream about.

However, the volume of meat that God intended to send wasn't to be a blessing but a burden. God planned to send enough meat for the people to eat until they were so sick of quail that they'd never want it again.

When I was in elementary school, I loved watermelon. It was my favorite food. Whenever I was at my grandmother's, she'd allow me to eat as much watermelon as I wanted. I remember one day when I ate an entire watermelon. I wasn't hungry at the time; I just ate it because I wanted it. But after that day, I couldn't stand watermelon anymore. What was meant for good turned into gross because my eyes had been bigger than my stomach.

Another time, when I was starting out in my career, I had my eyes on a corner office and promotion. While I tried to be grateful for my current job, I wanted the pay raise and prestige that came with a bigger title. But again, my eyes were too big for my stomach, so to speak. I did eventually get that corner office and pay raise and promotion—but much later in life. In God's mercy and grace, He allowed enough time and training to pass so that when the time came, I was ready for the stress, pressure, and responsibility that came along with that job in the corner office.

How often do we ask God to give us things in life not because we're prepared to receive them but because we aren't satisfied with what we already have?

Can you think of something you've been asking God for but you may not be ready to receive?

Perhaps you've been praying for a spouse, but are you ready to be a spouse? If you've been praying for more income, are you wisely handling the income that you already have? There are more sensitive prayer requests such as those for better health, protection for children, or wisdom to deal with elderly parents, and the question is whether you're fully trusting God with the resources and wisdom He has already given you, or you are still trying to do things on your own?

At first, Moses didn't understand why God was sending all of the quail. In Numbers 11:21, Moses questions how God could possibly provide six hundred thousand people with meat, but God says, basically, "I've got this" (v. 23). God wanted the Israelites to see a visual symbol of what an out-of-control hunger looked like. He wanted them to experience the fullness of their unfaithfulness and greed.

Read Numbers 11:31-34, and answer T (true) or F (false):

___T___ 1. God sent a wind to bring quail in from the sea.

___T___ 2. The people barely caught any quail.

___F___ 3. God was happy for the people as He watched them eat the quail.

Extra Insight

"Our fall was, has always been, and always will be, that we aren't satisfied in God and what He gives. We hunger for something more, something other."
—Ann Voskamp[9]

Imagine standing in the camp and looking off into the distance toward the Mediterranean Sea. There's a large, dark cloud moving toward shore. As you stand and observe the cloud, you realize that it's an enormous flock of birds coming your way. Since you've seen the migration before in Egypt, you know that quail are coming. Also, Moses had mentioned it the day before.

When you and your family lived in Egypt, your family likely ate dried, salted quail.[10] However, out in the wilderness, the thought of fresh roasted quail makes your mouth water. After all, it has been a while since you've had meat.

As the exhausted bevy of quail touched down on the shore, masses of your Israelite brothers and sisters ran toward the birds. Too tired to take flight, the birds shrill as greedy hands snatch them up and shove them into baskets, sheets, or whatever will hold the soon-to-be dinner. As the day goes on, quail are piled up two cubits, or three feet, high off the ground. Not every single person in camp gathers quail, but those who did really went for it. The least amount gathered among those who hoarded quail was ten homers, or sixty bushels, or almost two tons of quail. That's a lot of quail!

You watched the people roast the quail and eat. It had been a long time since the smell of cooking meat filled the air. At first, everyone was really excited. They ate like it was their last meal on earth. For some of them it was.

People started getting sick. Soon, masses of your neighbors and even some of your friends started dying—some even while they were still eating. The plague that struck the people might have been the result of spoiled, hoarded meat.[11] It's a shame that the people had forgotten the last time they hoarded food, when God sent His people manna each day, faithfully providing the food that they would need, but still they didn't trust His provision and hoarded the manna (see Exodus 16:20).

While we might have questionable feelings about the plague that God allowed to kill the people after they gorged themselves on quail, it's worth remembering that God gave the people what they wanted and allowed the consequences of their behavior. Sadly, the people's behavior revealed their greedy and unfaithful hearts.

Look up 1 Timothy 6:6 and write it below:

True Godiness is contentment

What does this verse mean to you, especially as it pertains to some of the "I wants" in your life? What do you have to gain by being content with whatever God has already given to you?

Knowing that God Provides what I need

Today's study ends on quite a heavy note. However, I believe that the account of the Israelites and the quail has substantial application to what we've been studying so far this week: it's only when we find our satisfaction in God that we can find real freedom.

Reflection Exercise

1. What is one takeaway from today's study?

Be satisfied ō what I have. What I eat, drink, cloth myself etc

2. In what area of your life do you need to honor God's provision and express more gratitude?

physical things

3. Is there a next step or action step that you feel God is prompting you to take today in order to honor Him more in your life?

Enjoy what I have Stop wishing for more

SURRENDER PRINCIPLE #2

I will live by faith rather than rush to follow my feelings.

Our feelings aren't wrong, but unchecked and unchallenged, they can lead us to do wrong things. So, what does it look like for us to not rush toward our feelings whenever they feel out of control and push us toward control-loving behaviors? Tomorrow we will explore that in detail.

This surrender principle is helpful to apply during those times when you get that surprise text message or phone call and you're tempted to react to whatever big emotion you're feeling in that moment. Our feelings scream "Fix it now!" while faith says, "Trust God's way."

What does this surrender principle mean to your life in what you're facing right now?

Prayer

Dear God, thank You for how You've provided what I need in my life. Lately, I haven't thanked You for <u>Paul's healing</u> *, so I want to express my gratitude for that right now. God, help me see the places in my life where I'm complaining so that I can repent and honor You with my words, my attitude, and my life. In Jesus' name. Amen.*

Day 4: Letting Go of Following Feelings

Historical records should have reflected the stellar career achievements of Naval Captain Lisa Nowak, a NASA astronaut who flew in the space shuttle in the summer of 2006. Instead, Nowak made national news as the woman who wore a disguise and an adult diaper to drive 950 miles to confront another woman who was involved with the same man as Nowak. In a confrontation at an airport, Nowak ended up spraying the other woman with pepper spray.[12] When she was arrested, authorities found items that led Nowak to be charged with attempted murder. Eventually she pled guilty to lesser charges, but her out-of-control behavior led to the loss of her career, among other losses.[13]

At the risk of reducing a complex situation to a simplistic explanation, I wonder what feelings drove her to such desperate measures to get what she wanted, even though she knew that it was wrong?

The title of today's study is intentional. Notice that it's letting go of "following feelings" rather than just letting go of "feelings." I want to make this distinction because God created our feelings, and those emotions are neither good nor bad. As author Chip Dodd writes, "Feelings…they are tools that we need to learn how to use well so that we do not behave impulsively and act out without the ability to take responsibility."[14]

Daily Surrender Prayer:

God, I choose to surrender

_____

_____

_____

to You today.

Today's study isn't about demeaning or dismissing our feelings. Whatever you feel is real, but today we'll explore why our feelings aren't always a reliable indicator of what we should or should not do.

When we talk about our feelings or emotions, we often describe them as residing in our "hearts."[15] When's the last time that you checked your heart? What are the emotions you've been feeling most often lately? How often do you feel like your emotions are bigger than your ability to handle them?

Our emotions are often launching pads for our actions. Lisa Nowak's story is an extreme tale about how control-loving behaviors plus strong feelings can lead to destructive outcomes. However, I've also experienced that strong feelings can fire up control-loving behaviors that lead us to try to fix or force our way to getting the love, peace, possession, purpose, or security we think we deserve.

Our feelings are real, but rushing to follow our feelings isn't wise.

In today's study, we'll look at how God guides us so that we don't rush to follow our feelings toward a negative response. Let's start with some of Scripture's best advice for our hearts.

Look up Proverbs 4:23 and write it below:

Above all else guard your heart
for everything you do flows from it.

The Hebrew word for heart is (leb)[18] which is a combination of our mind and our desires. The wisdom of this verse instructs us to pay attention and keep safeguards around what we think and feel because the direction of our lives flows from it.

What stands out to me is the word *guard* because I am aware that there are internal and external forces that can damage my heart. Last week, we looked at Jeremiah 17:9, which identifies that, apart from God, our hearts are the seat of deceit, so I've got to be aware of the damage that I can cause because my heart tends to be selfish and self-centered when I am not centered in Christ. I must also guard my heart against allowing Satan's lies or other words to hurt my heart.

What issues are affecting your heart the most these days?

Pride
that I always know best

What emotions are attached to those issues? Are there any emotions that are hard for you to control?

as above
maybe I need more
humility

leb (Hebrew)
mind + desires

maybe not?

There was a difficult period of my life when hurt, fear, and anger were strong and frequent emotions during our family crisis. In fact, on one very difficult day, I was involved in a very upsetting conversation that unleashed a torrent of fear running through my heart and mind. I grew so distressed at my lack of control over the situation that I picked up a number of dishes and hurled them through my kitchen window. Yes, you read that right. I am a Jesus-loving woman who lost control over her emotions and acted out in an embarrassing and epic way. It was awful. While this event happened years ago, I've never forgotten that if I don't guard my heart, I am still susceptible to following my feelings.

frustration
Remember
the
broken
chair
incident

Have you ever followed your feelings into a situation that resulted in pain, distress, or regret? If so, briefly describe what happened:

yelling @ Michael
losing control

There's a great visual illustration of God's presence with the Israelites in the wilderness from which we can draw some real and practical application. At the end of today's lesson, you're also going to engage in a powerful exercise to help you identify how emotions can trigger a negative response, leading to out-of-control or control-loving behaviors, or enable us to choose a positive response.

Read Numbers 9:15-17 and answer the following questions:

What covered the Tabernacle (holy place of meeting)? (v. 15)

cloud

At night, what did the cloud look like? (v. 16)

fire

When the cloud lifted, what did the Israelites do? (v. 17)

set out

When the cloud settled, what did the Israelites do? (v. 17)

encamped

The Israelites had seen a cloud guiding them before. God guided them with a pillar of cloud by day and a pillar of fire by night right after Pharaoh gave permission for them to go (see Exodus 13:21-22). Take a moment and consider how important God's guidance would have been for the people. They'd been enslaved for over four hundred years (Exodus 12:40), so the group likely didn't know where they were headed. After witnessing supernatural plagues, Pharaoh freed them. Imagine that! They were living under the control of the

Egyptians, and then they were free. Not only that; they had freedom without a real understanding of where they were going or what would happen next.

What kinds of emotions do you think the people might have been experiencing?

fear

anxiety

feeling out of control

The pillar of cloud and the pillar of fire existed to remind the people that God was with them. In verse 17, the word *settled* is *shakan*, which also means "dwell."[19] I love that God gave the people a visible reminder of His constant presence even though they would continue to struggle to trust God time and time again.

Read Numbers 9:22-23. How often did the people move?

when the cloud lifted

It varied a day, month a year

How did the people behave when God gave the command to move? (v. 23)

They moved

It's not often that we read positive news about the Israelites in the wilderness. It is so good to read that the Israelites were obedient when the cloud pillar moved.

I imagine that there may have been a few control-loving people in the Israelite camp who may have been tempted to strike out on their own and blaze a trail to the Promised Land without having to wait on the others.

Years ago, our family drove from Ohio to Florida to catch a cruise ship, and there was a giant debate over the number of bathroom breaks that we needed to agree upon before leaving. Some family members wanted to break as needed while other family members liked the idea of an adult astronaut diaper so that we could get there faster.

God used an external symbol to guide the Israelites and help them move toward His best for them. Now, we have the internal presence of the Holy Spirit dwelling in our hearts to help lead us in our lives.

There are several places where Jesus helps us see how the Holy Spirit living within us guides us and equips us to live, and also how to handle some of our human emotions that can get out of control if we are not intentional in responding appropriately.

Match the verse with the description or attribute of the Holy Spirit.

(c) John 16:12-14 (c)   a. Equips us to overcome sinful desires

(f) John 14:26 (f)   b. Prays for us when we can't pray

d. John 16:7   c. Guides us to the truth

d. 1 Corinthians 3:16   d. Lives inside of believers

(a) Galatians 5:16   e. Empowers us to live for God

g. Acts 1:8   f. Teaches us God's truth

b. Romans 8:26-27   g. Helps us

Remote Control versus Spirit Control

In my control-loving dreams, I wished that I could just point a remote control at people or situations and press a button to get what I wanted. Just point and click. Interestingly, I wouldn't want someone to try to make me do what I wasn't ready or willing to do. It's a hypocritical observation that I've got to own.

God's desire is for us to be controlled by His Spirit, not for us to control others or outcomes. Too many of us know that our efforts to control often ends badly; but when the Holy Spirit controls our lives, we experience freedom and peace.

Read Galatians 5:22-24. Write the individual aspects of the fruit of the Spirit in the blank spaces of the remote control.

How does the Holy Spirit help you let go and live like Jesus, responding to emotions in a healthy way, rather than follow your feelings into unhealthy or control-loving behaviors?

Lives in us to avoid giving into the flesh. Prays in us As all the above

love   joy

peace   fnbearance

kindness   goodness

faithfulness   gentleness

self-control

If we're going to deal with strong human emotions, it stands to reason that we're going to need the power of God living within us. That's why I am so grateful for God's Holy Spirit given to us when we accept Jesus Christ as our Savior and Lord.

As a child of God, redeemed by Jesus Christ, you have the power of God living within you to help you overcome negative responses to human hungers or desires in your life that can get out of control. No matter how hard it is for you to deal with your feelings or how out of control you might feel, God hasn't given up on you.

Read Philippians 1:6. How does this verse give you hope if you are feeling like a failure or hopeless?

That until "completion" => death or tn always until we see Jesus he will help carry us through

As you complete today's lesson, I want to make sure that you know it's okay to be real with how you feel. When you read my personal stories, I hope that you recognize that you aren't alone if you've responded inappropriately to some of your feelings. Life is complicated, but thankfully, you have God's Holy Spirit to empower you to respond to any of those eight emotions we outlined earlier in a way that glorifies God and blesses you.

Prayer

Healthy response Honest = conversations

Write a prayer in the margin acknowledging any feelings that have felt out of control lately, leading you toward an unhealthy response. Consider the role that the Holy Spirit plays in your life and invite Him to lead you toward His truth and healthy responses rather than to follow your feelings.

Day 5: Letting Go of Pacifiers

It doesn't take a newborn baby long to discover that food is good. God made babies with a strong sucking reflex. Very rarely does anyone have to teach a healthy baby how to nurse or take a bottle. Of course, when that newborn does what comes naturally, he or she is rewarded with milk.

It's no surprise that babies get a little upset when parents shift them from "feed on demand" to *scheduled* feedings. Babies get really unhappy when they want a meal but it isn't time to eat.

Enter the pacifier. At my house, we called it a "binky." It should have been called a "lifesaver." I hated it when my baby girls screamed like a lion was chasing them. Not only did I hate that they were unhappy, but the sound of their screaming in my ears didn't always feel so great either. Sometimes that pacifier seemed like the best and fastest way to make everyone happy, even if it was only for a little while.

While parents eventually wean their babies off of pacifiers, it's interesting that as adults we go looking for ways to pacify ourselves when we're hungry for something and are unable to get what we want. Even if what we're looking for only pacifies us for a little while, or even if it isn't good for us in the long term, what we want in that moment is just to feel better.

One of God's good purposes in the midst of our wilderness is to challenge our attempts to pacify ourselves. When we're in the wilderness, this is often a season when the hobby, the relationship, or the career that used to make us feel full and satisfied leaves us feeling empty and hungry. We may call out to God and beg Him to give us what we want, but if He allows us to stay in the wilderness, we sometimes take over and go looking for some pacifiers of our own.

What are some of those pacifiers? I like to describe them this way.

Whenever you're feeling emotionally, spiritually, or relationally starved, you're more likely to binge in one of these five areas. Place a checkmark beside the ones that resonate with you:

X **Binge-Eating—Consuming food to pacify the aching spaces within**

X **Binge-Spending—Buying stuff to replace what I can't get for myself**

_____ **Binge-Sleeping—Disengaging in hopes of escaping the pain**

_____ **Binge-Watching—Numbing my mind in front of movies, television, or social media**

X **Binge-Processing—Thinking and overthinking and rethinking situations**

A quick clarification: there's nothing sinful about eating food, buying things, taking a long nap, or looking at social media. The problem comes if you're using those things to pacify yourself for what you can't have in another area of your life. More than merely identifying our pacifiers, we need to ask ourselves, **How do I get to the point where I truly live as if God is all that I need?**

Shortly after leaving Egypt, God gave the Ten Commandments to Moses to take to the Israelites.

Look up Exodus 20:1-3 and write verse 3 below:

You shall have no other Gods betre me

Even Christians struggle with dependence on medications/ substances and battle addiction issues. If you aren't sure if you have a dependence or addiction, consider the following three questions:

1. Is there something that you are consuming each day to help you get through the day, calm down, or fall asleep?
2. Does the thought of giving up this thing make you anxious or afraid?
3. Are you keeping this a secret from others?

Extra Insight

Idols also can come in the form of self-image or self-preservation, the desire to control, or even fear, especially when fear makes us act or behave in a certain way.

In the NIV translation, the phrase "before me" can also be translated "besides me."

The pursuit or protection of even good things can become idols if we're not careful. In fact, what we love and care about most has the greatest potential to become an idol in our lives—even the things that started out as blessings that God gave us. One scholar defines an idol this way: "[It is] anything to which we devote our energy and time, or for which we make sacrifices because we love and serve it.... The idols that entice God's people today are things like money, recognition, success, material possessions (cars, houses, boats, collectibles), knowledge, or even other people."[20]

Is there anything in your life that you might have turned into an idol, making it difficult for you to fully surrender it (or him or her) to God?

Can you identify why you are holding on so tight?

*(handwritten note in margin: ** addiction to success in my children, the still academic success)*

In my life, my family became an idol for me, specifically the image of the family that I wanted the world to see. So, when addiction emerged in our household, threatening to break our family apart, I dedicated myself to trying to save my marriage and my family by any means necessary. But as I failed to see that I was powerless against the jaws of addiction, my dedication turned into desperation. Control-loving behaviors motivated not by love but by fear began to take over my life. Yes, I prayed and I surrendered in moments, but I spent a lot of time checking on God's progress and trying to help God out by trying to force solutions and fix those who didn't want to be fixed.

Just to be clear, it's not wrong to pray about family matters or to take responsible actions. We are invited to come boldly before God and ask for help (Hebrews 4:16). We're also instructed to use wisdom and gentleness to confront and assist fellow believers who've fallen into sin (Matthew 18:16-18; Galatians 6:1-2). However, the tipping point occurs when we become so focused on what we want—our dream—that we don't leave room for God to do things His way. That's when what we're trying to protect becomes an idol in our lives.

Once I admitted that my desire to fix my family had become an idol, I needed to surrender that desire or idol in order to leave space in my heart for God to take His rightful place at the forefront of my life. That's where that scary prayer came in: *God, I want You to be all that I need.* In order for me to do that, I had to surrender my idol.

Satisfaction = not wanting any more

There in my prayer closet over many months, I chose to daily open my hands. This was an act of surrender. *I know that what I'm saying may feel really scary for you right now, but keep going!* I had to give what I couldn't fix or handle any longer to God, allowing Him to guide the outcome. As I prayed with my open hands in my lap and tears streaming down my face, I decided to trust Him for whatever He would leave in my hands and continue to trust Him even if He allowed what I loved and cherished to be removed. Was it scary? Yes! I couldn't do this on my own, but with God all things are possible. Each day as I prayed that prayer, the grip of fear loosened. As I came with open hands to God each day, He filled my life with His power, His provision, and His peace. He was more than enough!

As Jesus taught and talked to the hurting, broken, lost, and suffering, He invited them to replace their idols or "pacifiers" with a satisfying connection with Him.

Read John 4:4-14, and answer the following questions:

Jesus stopped by Jacob's well because He was ___*tired*___ .

Why was the Samaritan woman surprised that Jesus would ask her for a drink?

Because Jews did not associate ā Samaritans.

What did Jesus tell her that He had to offer?

living water

Write verses 13-14 in your own words:

Jesus gives us living water so we can have eternal life

– find satisfaction in Jesus

Jesus talks with a Samaritan woman who'd been thirsty for more than just water in her life. As Jesus strikes up a conversation with her, the woman admits to five husbands and another relationship with a man who wasn't her husband. We don't know the details of her life story, but it's possible that somewhere along the line those husbands weren't enough for what she was looking for in life. Rather than condemn her life choices, Jesus spoke to the woman's greater need: to find satisfaction in Him. ✓

In John 6, we read that Jesus performed the miracle of feeding the five thousand and a few people tracked Him down because they were impressed

Our souls must be surrendered to Christ before we can find satisfaction in Christ.

with what He'd done. However, Jesus elaborates on the spiritual lesson of lasting satisfaction rather than just being full after eating a few loaves and several fish.

Read John 6:30-35 and complete the following.

Who or what is Jesus referring to in verse 33?

himself

Write verse 35 below, and underline the word *comes*.

Then Jesus declared, "I am the bread of life. Whoever comes to me will never go hungry

A few verses later, in John 7, Jesus secretly traveled to Judea to attend the Festival of the Tabernacles. He went secretly because He knew that the Jewish leaders were looking for a way to kill him. Halfway through the festival, Jesus stood up in the temple courts and began to teach (John 7:14). At first the people listening were amazed. Then things got dicey because the people in the crowds were arguing over who Jesus was. Yet there were receptive hearts in the audience.

Read John 7:37-38 below, and underline the phrase "come to me."

[37]On the last and greatest day of the festival, Jesus stood and said in a loud voice, "Let anyone who is thirsty <u>come to me</u> and drink. [38] Whoever believes in me, as Scripture has said, rivers of living water will flow from within them."

(John 7:37-38)

What was the invitation that Jesus gave to the crowd?

To believe in him

What would flow within them?

living water

On the seventh day of the festival, there was a special ceremony with a water-pouring and torch-lighting display. These were symbols of water in the desert and meaningful to help the people remember how God sustained those wilderness wanderers long ago.[22]

On the eighth day, there would be no water-pouring, so Jesus' words to the crowd would have grabbed their attention because they were reflecting on a time when water was scarce and provisions were low, and he was proclaiming that he would be a source of never-ending supply.

As Jesus spoke to the Samaritan woman, the five thousand people He fed, and the crowd at the festival, He invited people to come to Him for what would satisfy.

I find it interesting that I often feel like I have to chase down what I think will satisfy me. Yet Jesus offers to give us lasting satisfaction. In Christ, there is fulfillment when we come and ask Jesus for it. The more we ask for the satisfaction that Jesus offers, the more we receive. The more we receive, the more satisfied our souls are. In fact, the Hebrew word for "soul" is *nephesh*.[23] As I looked at the different definitions of the word, I noticed that *soul* was equivalent to *passion* and *appetite*. It follows that whatever we feed our souls will determine our appetites.

So, what does it look like to come to Jesus to satisfy? For that, the psalmist provides a visual lesson.

Read Psalm 42:1-2 in the margin. What image is used here for "satisfaction"?

Streams of water

The writer observes how deer will journey long and far to find water. God embedded an instinct in deer to prioritize finding water for survival. While humans also need water for survival, we're often distracted from consuming water because we've got other choices to drink. Deer don't have to deal with all of the different choices that we do; or maybe they do have choices and they always choose what's best.

Many of us came to Jesus for salvation. Yet how often do we forget throughout the week to come to Him for a fresh supply of living water to sustain us in a world that offers only sugary substitutes? *Why do I not come to you oh Lord*

Read Psalm 107:9 and Isaiah 58:11 in the margin. What will God do for those who desire satisfaction in Him?

guide me
strengthen me
satisfy me

Reflection Exercise

As you reflect on how often you come to Christ to seek living water to satisfy your soul, answer the following:

---

[1] *As the deer pants for streams of water,*
so my soul pants for you, my God.
[2] *My soul thirsts for God, for the living God.*
When can I go and meet with God?
(Psalm 42:1-2)

The Lord will guide you always;
he will satisfy your needs in a sun-scorched land and will strengthen your frame.
You will be like a well-watered garden, like a spring whose waters never fail.
(Isaiah 58:11)

For he satisfies the thirsty and fills the hungry with good things.
(Psalm 107:9)

1. How does your time with God—whether in Bible study, prayer, worship, or silent meditation—satisfy you?

2. If you don't feel satisfied after spending time with God in one of these ways, have you identified any of the reasons why? What could make it more satisfying?

3. After today's study, do you sense God asking you to think or behave differently in any area?

Help me understand our role in HF to build patients support physician practice grow practice provide patients c sense of caring

Use my words ... explain Play c concentration - Not the drs by kind.

Imagine trading your desperate "I wants" for experiencing satisfaction in God's presence, love, and power in your life. Rather than feeling overwhelmed by what you don't or can't have, you would overflow with peace, joy, and the assurance that you have everything you need. I hope that this is your heart's desire!

Prayer

Dear God, I want You to be all that I need. Today I want to lay down anything or anyone that I've put before You. While I know that You invite me to pray to You about what's going on in my life, I don't want my desires to become more important than my desire for You. In Jesus' name. Amen.

Bonus Exercise: Figure Your Trigger

What are some of the triggers that prompt you to go looking for a pacifier? It might be helpful to do a little digging, and it's okay to acknowledge that you may be challenging the very thing that is helping you cope in an uncomfortable season of life. The following exercise guides you in identifying the emotions and behaviors that send you in search of a pacifier.

Romans 8:1 reminds us that there is no condemnation for those who are in Christ. So, if binge behavior has gotten out of control in your life, God is waiting for you to acknowledge it and invite Him to bring freedom and victory to that part of your life.

Step 1: Identify Triggers and Triggering Behaviors

Complete the sections that apply to your life now. If you don't feel comfortable filling them out in your workbook, then grab a separate sheet of paper and complete the exercise. You need to complete only the sections that apply to you.

I strongly encourage you to consider sharing with the other ladies in your group if you feel that you can share in confidence. You'll discover that you aren't alone in your struggle!

BINGE EATING

I am tempted to *binge eat* by consuming ___Chocolate___

(favorite comfort foods)

when I feel ___Sad + anxious___

(name emotions)

or after _____

(difficult event/action)

or after I interact with _____

(name person/people).

IMPACT: I do this because it helps me to feel
___happy___,

but this behavior is costing me because
___fatness___.

BINGE BUYING/SHOPPING

I am tempted to *binge shop* by purchasing

_____

(unnecessary/extra items you impulsively order)

when I feel _____

(name emotions)

or after _____

(difficult event/action)

or after I interact with _____

(name person/people).

IMPACT: I do it because it helps me to feel

_____,

but this behavior is costing me because:

_____.

BINGE WATCHING

I am tempted to *binge watch* _____

(names of TV/streaming media/

social media)

for _____

(how long do you spend watching)

when I feel _____

(name emotions)

or after _____

(difficult event/action)

or after I interact with _____

(name person/people).

IMPACT: I do it because it helps me to feel

_____,

but this behavior is costing me because:

_____.

BINGE SLEEPING

I am tempted to *binge sleep* or lie around and do nothing

when I feel _____

(name emotions)

or after I _____

(difficult event/action)

or after I interact with _____

(name person/people).

Write a Bible verse that you can recall when tempted to binge watch:

Write a Bible verse that you can recall when tempted to binge sleep or numb yourself:

IMPACT: I do it because it helps me to feel

_____,

but this behavior is costing me because:

_____.

As you reflect on this exercise, are there any common triggers that you are now aware of?

Step 2: *Move toward Freedom*

If you struggle with binging on certain things after an emotional trigger, follow Jesus' example by invoking God's Word.

For each trigger, grab a note card or sticky note and write Matthew 4:4 on the card and the verse that you wrote in the related box above. I suggest that you tape the card to whatever your pacifier might be, whether a favorite kind of cookie or chip, your credit card, or on the front of your television or computer. If your mobile device aids you in pacifying your hunger, then consider programming those same verses into an alarm on your phone during the times of day that you're tempted to binge. The goal is to unleash God's power against your pull toward your pacifier.

Accountability: _____ I completed Step 2.

That we don't live by bread alone but by every word!

Step 3: *Transfer Your Trigger*

As helpful as I hope this exercise is for you, those triggers still exist. It's so helpful to identify your triggers and Step 2 gives you a practical next step to begin addressing your trigger. Now, it's time to transform your trigger and redirect your next steps from binging to behaviors that are life-giving instead of shame-inducing.

When you begin to feel a temptation toward one of your triggers, here are four ways to redirect your actions:

1. Take a walk—Remove yourself from the trigger and the pacifier.
2. Phone a friend—Let someone you trust know that you're feeling tempted.

3. Deep breathing—Inhale deeply and repeat the Bible verses that you identified to overcome your trigger.
4. Practice gratitude—Using both hands, list ten blessings in your life.

Any other ideas? _____

Prayer

Dear God, thank You for Jesus' example when He was faced with temptation. Thank You for the life-giving power of Your truth to fill my heart, mind, and soul with lasting satisfaction. God, I am praying over the next steps that You want me to take when it comes to identifying my emotional triggers. I want to glorify You in everything that I say and do. Give me the courage to take the necessary next steps so that I can let go of my pacifiers and find my satisfaction only in You. Amen!

Numbers 11:18-23

Numbers 11:31-32

the Quail
story

Wilderness principles
ABC
a) we are
always
loved

Surrender Principle #2

We choose to live by ___faith___

not rush to follow our ___feelings___.

b) God is
always fn
us

ONLY JESUS SATISFIES!!

Matthew 4:2 — It is written, Man shall not live on bread alone, but on every word that comes from the mouth of God

c) trust God

Hebrews 2:14 — Jesus knows what it looks like to live in flesh

We are satisfied when we set our hearts on God's ___priorities___

versus our ___plans___

* In the wilderness

Hebrews 4:12 — For the word of God is alive + active and sharper than any double edge sword

Joshua 1:8 — Keep this book of the Law always on our lips

D - God's word designed as our design God's nature — native wilderness, word aspirations reshapes our aspirations DNA

We are satisfied when we decide that only ___Jesus___

will ___satisfy___ us. The wilderness allows us to reflect on what God wants for us

day + night!! That we think about it day + night + that we follow it!!

Then you will be prosperous + successful

Week 3

Letting Go of Circumstances

(Matthew 4:5-7)

Memory Verse

[There's] a right time to hold on and another to let go.
(Ecclesiastes 3:6 MSG)

"Are you sick?"

That's the question my sister whispered in my ear Thanksgiving night five years ago. She had good reason to ask.

I wasn't sick, but in a matter of weeks, I'd dropped an alarming and noticeable amount of weight from my real-woman frame. That weight loss was just one symptom of a woman who'd lost control before spiraling out of control.

Three weeks before, a failed addiction intervention had taken place in my home. As I was planning the intervention, I knew that I was rushing the process; however, the pain that addiction had brought into our lives pushed me to draw a line in the sand. I thought that I'd done everything I could to ensure my desired outcome to get a loved one's life back on track. The final scene of zipping suitcases, slamming doors, and angry accusations proved otherwise. It was purely awful.

Yet that didn't stop me from doubling down my efforts to try to fix the situation. I activated every control-loving behavior I could to try and fix a situation that was most definitely out of my control.

Ultimately, God redeemed that devastating circumstance by fixing the broken spiritual beliefs and attitudes inside of *me*. As God began to transform my heart and mind, I learned to open my hands and let go of trying to fix a situation in hopes of securing my vision of what a happy outcome looked like. As a result, instead of begging for a particular outcome, I've learned to ask for God's best, even if there is pain and hurt involved. This isn't an easy journey, but I promise that it's worth it!

This week in our study we see that Satan challenges Jesus to act outside of God's promises by forcing God to rescue Him. However, Jesus possessed complete clarity around who He was and what He came to do. That clarity equipped Jesus to avoid testing God and instead trust God with the trajectory of his life, even though He knew that the outcome of His time on earth would come with great pain and suffering.

Day 1: Tempted with Half Truths

In today's study, we're going to examine how Satan used Scripture in an attempt to fool Jesus with a half-truth in order to tempt Him to force God to rescue Him and protect Him

God, I choose to surrender <u>my diet</u>

_____

to You today.

Extra Insights

Herod the Great ordered a massive temple of shining white stone to be built starting in 19 BC. It was built on the same site as Solomon's and Zerubbabel's temples hundreds of years before.[2] The entire structure wasn't completed until AD 64 and it was destroyed by the Romans in AD 70.[3]

_____

"We tempt God when we 'force' Him (or dare Him) to act contrary to His Word."[4]

from harm. As you move through this week's study, you'll see that this particular temptation is all about our human desire to force God to follow our agenda or to assume He will rescue us from any situation we might find ourselves in. Your goal is to <u>learn how to live like Jesus and move toward trusting God's ultimate plan for you and those whom you care about.</u>

how to live like Jesus + move toward trusting God

Read Matthew 4:5-7 and Luke 4:9-10, and answer the following questions:

In what city does Jesus' next temptation take place?

Jerusalem

How did Jesus get there?

the devil led him

What did Satan tempt Jesus to do?

throw himself off a mountain → *really the rest of the point* *of the temple*

In a plot twist, Satan takes Jesus from the wilderness to Jerusalem and places Him on the highest point of the temple. What's shocking to me is that Jesus allows Satan to continue tempting Him from a different location.

Why do you think Jesus allowed Satan to take Him to another location to be tempted?

To show us how to walk through temptation

As we've read before, Jesus experiences suffering during His wilderness temptation; but rather than reject being subjected to more pain, He chooses to identify with our pain. Jesus could have taken control of the situation at any moment, but He doesn't. Instead, He shows us how to walk and live in victory over our circumstances.

Both Matthew's and Luke's accounts of this second temptation are identical; however, in Matthew, this is listed as the second temptation. In Luke, this is listed as the third temptation. It's not known why Luke listed the record of events in such a way, but one scholar notes that Matthew's use of "then" between the first and second temptation indicates the correct order of events.[1]

No longer in the wilderness, Jesus now stands at the highest point of the temple, known as Herod's Temple, commissioned by Herod the Great. The "pinnacle of the temple" would have been about 450 feet above the Kidron Valley below. A few years later, Jesus and his disciples would cross through the Kidron Valley on their way to garden of Gethsemane where Jesus would be arrested before he was crucified (John 18:1).

As Jesus stands at the top of the temple, Satan proposes that if Jesus throws himself off the highest point of the temple, then angels would save him. To back up his pitch, Satan references Scripture and begins his recitation with, "It is written," the same phrase that Jesus used in Matthew 4:4 to overcome the first temptation. Then Satan proceeds to quote Psalm 91:11-12; however, he twists the Scripture to fit his agenda.

Look up Psalm 91:11-12 and write it below.

For he will command his angels concerning you to guard you in all your ways. They will lift you up in their hands so you will not strike your foot against a stone.

Compare Psalm 91:11-12 to Satan's response to Jesus. What phrase does Satan leave out?

It's sobering to realize that Satan also knows the Scriptures. What's helpful to remember is that Satan lies 100 percent of the time, but we must be able to identify his lies. God's almighty power and purposes will ultimately prevail against evil, but Satan knows that in the meantime, he can deceive and confuse God's people with half-truths. In this case, Satan left out a key phrase, and you will discover the implications of that omission in tomorrow's study.

As a young boy, Jesus learned the ancient texts and memorized the words so that He would know how to avoid half-truths and deceptions when He heard them. Even after forty days and forty nights in the wilderness and the pressure of great hunger, Jesus didn't waver in what He knew to be true. Rather than a leap of faith, it would have been a leap of foolishness for Him to yield to Satan's temptation because it would have meant acting in opposition to God's plan for Him.

Why do people get confused or led astray by false teaching or half-truths? Here's a sobering message that Paul wrote his coworker Timothy. He warned that influential people, including elders within the church, will rise up and teach deceptive doctrines (Acts 20:28-31). Paul wanted to warn Timothy about what would happen as a result.

Read 1 Timothy 4:1-2 and 2 Timothy 4:3-4 in the margin. What does Paul say would happen to people in later times? Who would lead them astray?

People who tell them what they want to hear

Rather than teaching the gospel that calls people to faith and freedom in Christ, false teachers skillfully manipulate Scripture to deceive others. Their

[1]The Spirit clearly says that in later times some will abandon the faith and follow deceiving spirits and things taught by demons. [2]Such teachings come through hypocritical liars, whose consciences have been seared as with a hot iron.

(1 Timothy 4:1-2)

[3]For a time is coming when people will no longer listen to sound and wholesome teaching. They will follow their own desires and will look for teachers who will tell them whatever their itching ears want to hear. [4]They will reject the truth and chase after myths.

(2 Timothy 4:3-4 NLT)

goal is to woo people away from serving Christ and serve their own selfish agendas instead.

It's a little scary to read about people being deceived and led astray. So, a question you might ask is, "How do I make sure that I'm not being led astray or deceived?" Great question! There's a group of people who model what you can do whenever you hear someone teaching from the Bible.

Read Acts 17:10-12. What did the Bereans do after hearing someone teach from the Scriptures?

They examined the Scriptures

I love picturing this scene of believers who heard an apostle or another believer teach and then would get together after hearing the message and search the Scriptures to make sure that what was taught lined up with the ancient text.

The best way to identify a lie is to know the truth. However, when you're not sure about what's true, deception has an opening to begin wiggling in a lie.

It's natural to question your faith and what you believe about God during tough times or when you're feeling insecure or confused. That's a good thing! However, just like you make sure that you've got accurate directions when you're leaving for a road trip, you'll want to exercise wisdom and discernment on where you go looking for answers. There are a lot of people proposing answers and solutions who sound like Christians, but their answers actually lead people on a path far from God. We're most vulnerable to these messengers when we're facing trials or feeling confused or hurting.

During long wilderness seasons, I've questioned every single belief that I've had about faith and trusting God. Here are three lessons that I've learned:

1. My questions, or even my confusion, do not undermine God's power and sovereignty.
2. My feelings alone can't and should not shape my faith. Balance is critical when it comes to faith development and spiritual growth.
3. I must be careful about who I allow to influence my beliefs, especially when I'm in pain or feeling vulnerable.

Which one of those lessons is meaningful to you right now?

It's okay to feel big feelings! Don't be discouraged by your anger, sadness, grief, or confusion. You don't have to deny those feelings, but I want to encourage you to remain ruthless in focusing on God's character, holiness, and promises. As John 8:32 says, when you know the truth, the truth will set you free!

Memory Verse Reflection

[There's] a right time to hold on and another to let go.
(Ecclesiastes 3:6 MSG)

What does Ecclesiastes 3:6 mean to you?

This week's memory verse is taken from an ancient text written long ago by the wisest man in human history, King Solomon. Toward the end of his life, Solomon reflected on how he lived and the world around him. Ecclesiastes captures the king's reflections.

Part of our struggle with giving over or surrendering is that we don't often agree with God's time line for what must come or go in our lives. While this verse alludes to a "right time," that doesn't always line up with what we'd designate as "our time." Yet throughout the pages of Scripture, there are quite a few places where we read that "at the right time" God changed the game because He had something better for us than what was before.

This week's memory verse symbolizes the beginning of the letting go journey that I hope you will choose to take with me. Letting go might seem impossible because you've been holding on for so long, but that's only part of the journey. We're going to learn what it looks like to live like Jesus, who walked faithfully in hard times and left behind a beautiful footprint for us to follow toward surrender and blessed freedom.

Prayer

Dear God, while it's always hard to admit that I am not in control, I am so grateful that You are! So, I choose to surrender my attempts to control _WORK_ —> *Please guide me* today. Only You can handle, change, or fix that situation; and so I am giving it over to You. I trust that You will do what's best and right for Your glory and my good. In Jesus' name. Amen.

Day 2: My Way or God's Way

There's one story in the Bible that sobers me like none other. Maybe it's because I could see myself in the same situation making the exact same mistake. The following wilderness story is the background context for Jesus' response to Satan's second temptation. This story captures what happens when we know what God has called us to do and yet we want to do it our own way or in our own time.

In Numbers 20, the Israelites complain to Moses about the lack of water. Again. (Moses has put up with a lot of complaining and grumpy people.) In the past, God gave Moses instructions on how to bring about safe drinking water for the complaining people. This situation is no different. In Numbers 20:8, God tells Moses to take his staff (a large stick symbolizing authority and leadership) and speak to a rock that was before the people. Then enough water would flow to satisfy the entire Israelite community and their animals.

Moses grabs his staff and gathers the people in front of the rock. However, in verse 10, Moses says some alarming words: "Listen, you rebels, must we bring you water out of this rock?" Rather than standing before the people and proclaiming that God was about to send a provisional miracle to meet their needs, it almost sounds as if Moses is taking credit for what was about to happen.

Then, instead of speaking to the rock, Moses struck the rock, not once, but twice with his staff. This was not what God instructed him to do.

While water flowed from the rock and the Israelites drank their fill, Moses failed to follow God in obedience. He also failed to give God glory for their provision. Instead, Moses tossed out God's plan in favor of an anger-driven reaction to the people's complaining. While the people of Israel had no idea that Moses was disobedient, Moses knew. And God knew. And as we will see, there would be consequences.

This story hits close to home because I am aware that in the "frustration wilderness" I am easily tempted to seek my own solutions or take credit for God's provision. In doing so, God may allow my efforts to be successful, but there are spiritual and relational consequences for taking God's plan and doing it my way.

Today we're going to explore the next part of Satan's plan—to tempt Jesus to force God's hand—as well as Jesus' rebuttal of Satan's tactic. As we reflect on this next temptation, we'll be challenged to consider what it means to stay faithful to God's agenda, fighting the temptation to run off and follow our own.

Read Matthew 4:5-7. How does Jesus begin his rebuttal to Satan?

do not put the Lord your God to the test

Jesus quotes from Deuteronomy 6:16. Look up that verse and write it below:

Do not put the Lord you God to the test

Extra Insight

The word *Massah* means "testing."

The verse Jesus quotes from Deuteronomy refers to another event that happened to the Israelites in the wilderness when they were upset about not having enough water.

Read Exodus 17:1-7, and summarize what happened below:

Water is necessary for survival. The symbolism of God providing water as a means of continuing life for the Israelites in the wilderness is so powerful. As I reflect on the Scripture that Jesus used and the events behind that verse, I notice that the provision of water in the Old Testament is a mirror symbol of Jesus' proclamation that He is our source of eternal living water in the New Testament.

Exodus 17:1-7 records another instance of the Israelites' anger over not having water, even though God had provided water multiple times before. At Massah, a frustrated Moses goes to God for help. God tells him to go out in front of the people and strike the rock with the staff. Moses followed God's instructions and water came out. However, these are the final words of verse 7: "They tested the LORD saying, 'Is the LORD among us or not?'"

As you reflect on verse 7, why did the Israelites' attitude test God?

The Israelites experienced God's provision time and time again in the wilderness, yet they grumbled because they weren't getting what they wanted when they wanted it. The irony is that God had told them that they would encounter trials to see if they would believe whether or not He would sustain them in the wilderness (Exodus 15:22-27).

Of all the places where Satan could have taken Jesus, he took Jesus to the highest point of the temple. It would be here that any move Jesus made would be visible and would cause a scene in front of God's people below. Here, Satan tempts Jesus to jump and create the possibility that God would command the angels to conduct a spectacular mid-air save. Basically, Satan tempts Jesus to force God to save Him from a self-willed action. So, in quoting Exodus 17 back to Satan, Jesus basically is saying, "I know that people in the past have tried to force God's hand in hard times, but I'm standing here in faith, ultimately trusting in God's heart."

Look again at the phrase from Psalm 91:11-12 that Satan left out of his recitation of Matthew 4:6, which you recorded in yesterday's lesson on page 85. Write the phrase again below:

The phrase "to guard you in all your ways" means full and complete obedience to what God calls us to do and 100 percent submission to God's path and plan. Perhaps one of the most powerful invitations we can accept during trials or long seasons of difficulty is the invitation to leave "Cafeteria Christianity," or the picking and choosing of how and when we'll follow God, and decide to trust God in all of His ways.

Let's explore an example of this that probably hits home for many of us: You and I have people in our lives we'd love to see respond to Jesus' offer of salvation. While the Bible instructs us to always be ready to give an answer for the hope that we have (1 Peter 3:15), there are times when we take God's command to make disciples and attempt to lead people to Jesus by using control-loving tactics in the name of following that command. I believe this happens when we force people to come to church or nag someone to read the Bible or attend a small group with us.

Does God need our control-loving tactics to accomplish His purposes? Are there people in your home, workplace, neighborhood, or even your church with whom you're using control-loving behaviors in hopes of getting them into a relationship with God? If so, write about it briefly below:

5 Trust in the LORD with all your heart and lean not on your own understanding; 6 in all your ways submit to him, and he will make your paths straight. (Proverbs 3:5-6)

Read Proverbs 3:5-6 in the margin. Underline the portion of Scripture that matches Psalm 91:11.

Submission is agreeing to follow someone. Contrary to what many mistakenly believe, submission is a free-will decision. Jesus willingly submitted to God's plan to save humanity (see Philippians 2:7-8). Jesus came to give His life for humanity, not create circumstances requiring God to save His life from acts of self-interest. He successfully challenged Satan's temptation because Jesus had clarity about who He was and what God called Him to do. With that in mind, Jesus gives us instructions on who we're called to be and what we're called to do.

Read Mark 12:30-31 and summarize Jesus' two commandments for your life:

1. _____Love_____ God

2. _____love_____ Others

When we're feeling desperate, our desire to regain control can create distance between us and God. The farther we move from God and live without the influence and power of the Holy Spirit, the more we'll struggle to love others in a way that is healthy or helpful. Let's be honest; even when we feel close to God, loving others can be a challenge. We need to keep God in the top spot of our lives; otherwise, we'll jump in the top spot and try to make others serve our selfish needs for love and acceptance.

Reflection Exercise:

1. **What are or have been some of God's ways or instructions that you've struggled to totally obey or completely surrender to?**

   Trusting God's ability to keep me safe @ work ovo emotionally & financially

2. **Can you identify a time when you knew what God was calling you to do but you decided to do it your way? If so, write about it briefly:**

   I tried to become a teacher

3. **Is there a step of faith that you sense God might be leading you to take?**

   Not sure

Before you read the final prayer in today's study, I encourage you stop and take a deep breath. Those reflection questions may poke at a tender or fearful place in your heart or mind. It's okay if there are places where you're still working

Half-truths appeal to our desire to find the wiggle room in Scripture so that we can figure out how to get what we want if we're concerned that God won't give it to us.

on trusting God with all of your heart. If there is a step of faith that you feel led to take, but you aren't sure how to do it or need more support in order to do it, reach out to your group leader or a trusted Christian friend.

Prayer

Dear God, I want to honor You in all of my ways, no matter what I am facing. As I reflect on how I'm doing when it comes to living out love toward You and others, help me to get to the bottom of any root of fear or selfishness that is influencing my behavior today. In Jesus' name. Amen.

Day 3: Letting Go of Fear

Daily Surrender Prayer:

God, I choose to surrender

—————————

—————————

—————————

to You today.

God, grant me the serenity to accept the things I cannot change,
Courage to change the things I can,
And the wisdom to know the difference.
—*"Serenity Prayer," attributed to Reinhold Neibuhr*

In standing up against Satan's second temptation, Jesus taught us that we can trust God in the timing of trials of our lives. We don't have to be afraid or try to control others or steer an outcome away from an uncertain or unhappy ending on the horizon.

Every Saturday morning for many years, I've sat in a plastic chair in an anonymous community of people whom I only know by their first name. We begin each meeting repeating the "Serenity Prayer." In that room, I listen and learn from the experiences, strength, and hope of others who have lived with or loved someone fighting an addiction. As I've added my recovery experience to what I've learned through studying God's Word, prayer, and other spiritual practices, it has been such a blessing to move away from the chaos of control-loving behaviors to a life of calm and peace—even though our situation continued to get worse.

My only regret is that I didn't walk into those rooms sooner. Fear kept me away.

I was afraid to admit that addiction was part of our family.

I feared what would happen to my family.

I feared failure.

I feared not having any control to change our situation.

I feared what other people would think.

Over the years, I've come to discover that fear is like a brick. Each time we experience fear or think about what we're afraid of, those thoughts are like bricks that build up in our hearts and minds. The more we think of our fears, the more those bricks become like walls that crowd in on us, making us more afraid and closing us off from reaching out for help.

When we allow something to surround us and close us in, that's called a stronghold. Many of us are trapped by a stronghold of fear in our lives. "Strongholds in this context are wrong thoughts and perceptions contradicting the true knowledge of God and the nature of God."[6] If we want to break down the stronghold of fear, then we need the power of God's truth to tear down those walls.

Today we're going to talk about letting go of our fear-filled thoughts and choosing to allow the power of God to tear down the strongholds of fear in our lives.

On the bricks below, write some of the fears that you can't stop thinking about or that you often try to control—or perhaps escape or flee from.

Job

health, power's & children's
mind lives

Grandchildren   my children's faith   my power or position   money

am I an imposter   do I know enough

If you don't have a lot of fears, great! But for those who are struggling with fear, let's begin with some reassurances from God's Word.

Look up the following verses and summarize the encouragement or promise found in each:

Jeremiah 29:11

I know the plans I have for you declares the Lord. Plans to prosper you & not bring you harm

Matthew 6:34

don't worry about tomorrow

Psalm 46:1

God is our refuge + strength, an ever present help in trouble

1 Peter 5:7

Cast all my anxiety on him because he cares for you

Fear never goes down without a fight! Let's look at what happens to those around us when we don't deal with our fear. Our case study features the Israelites in the wilderness, and they use their fear for their children as an excuse to rebel against God.

One of the most powerful illustrations of the stronghold of fear occurs in Numbers 13. The scene unfolds as the twelve spies who Moses sent to scout the Promised Land returned and gave their report to the leaders and people of Israel. Ten of the spies talked about giants that would defeat the Israelites (Numbers 13:31-33). Only two spies, named Joshua and Caleb, reminded the people of God's faithfulness and promises.

Unfortunately, fear drove the people to listen to the ten men. As you read the following verses, pay attention to how the people's fear caused them to behave.

Read Numbers 14:1-10, and answer the following questions:

What are the people afraid will happen to their wives and children? (v. 3)

they will be taken as plunder by the Giants + people of the land

What were the reasons that Joshua and Caleb told the people that they didn't have to be afraid? (vv. 8-9)

the Lord would provide + give us a land flowing ū milk + honey

How did the people respond to Joshua and Caleb's report? (v. 10)

they want to stone them

God had put up with a lot of complaining and unfaithfulness from the Israelites during their short time in the wilderness. He had prepared a new home for them, and they flatly rejected it, using their fear for their families as an excuse to rebel against God. While God forgives the people at Moses' request (Numbers 14:20), God still punishes them for their rebellion. This is the incident that led God to sentence the Israelites to wander in the wilderness for forty years, and no one over the age of twenty at the time of the rebellion would enter the Promised Land (Numbers 14:29).

Has there ever been a time when your fear about something or someone caused you to sin or affected your relationship with God?

The Israelites faced an ongoing battle to trust that God would take care of them. We face that common fear too. However, a game-changer occurs when we are convinced of God's love for us.

Read 1 John 4:18 in the margin. What is not a part of love?

fear

> There is no fear in **love**. But **perfect love** drives out fear, because fear has to do with punishment. The one who fears is not made **perfect** in **love**.
>
> *(1 John 4:18, emphasis added)*

What is a reason or cause behind fear?

Not getting what we want or we think is best

The good news for all of us is that we're not facing a life sentence in a stronghold of fear!

Read 2 Corinthians 10:3-4 in the margin. What kind of weapons do we have to demolish strongholds?

divine power God!!

> [3]For though we live in the world, we do not wage war as the world does. [4]The weapons we fight with are not the weapons of the world. On the contrary, they have divine power to demolish strongholds.
>
> *(2 Corinthians 10:3-4)*

Paul uses war metaphors here; perhaps he was thinking about Roman military equipment such as first-century catapults, battering rams, and even an ancient version of a mechanical ladder.[7] He would have seen the evidence of enemy strongholds that had been destroyed. Paul wants us to know that we've got divine fighting power at our disposal too! Think about that for a moment. Imagine seeing all of the fear bricks that are surrounding and weighing down your heart being destroyed. Your fear of not being able to pay rent each month...boom! Gone. Your daily fear of not having health insurance...kapow! Your fears about your kids getting hurt...boom!

God's power can destroy your strongholds of fear. But how?

> We demolish arguments and every pretension that sets itself up against the knowledge of God, and we take captive every thought to make it obedient to Christ.
>
> *(2 Corinthians 10:5)*

Read 2 Corinthians 10:5 in the margin. How do we destroy our wrong thoughts?

By being obedient to Christ

What does it mean to make our thoughts obedient to Christ?

trust   prayer
faith

One commentator imagines Paul to be like a Roman military commander who is rounding up enemy prisoners and making them bow before God.[8] I connect with this imagery because I have found great freedom in admitting all of my fearful thoughts, temptations, and doubts to God. Whatever we don't surrender to God has the potential to become a stronghold in our lives. Since strongholds are hard to tear down once built, our best way forward is to keep them from being built by following Paul's wisdom and taking each individual thought captive.

Take a moment and imagine taking your fears from that imaginary brick stronghold and putting handcuffs on them. Label three fears below.

_____job_____   __children__   _& grand_
                    paul's death   *children*

Now put those fears "under arrest" and tell them that, by the authority given to you in Jesus Christ, they no longer have the power to mess with your thought life. If you need words to pray, here are some words below:

"Listen up, you _____ (name those fears) are under arrest in Jesus' name! You no longer have power over me because I've already got victory in Jesus' name (John 16:33), I know that Almighty God fights for me (Exodus 13:14), and with God all things are possible (Matthew 28:19)."

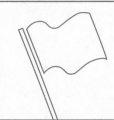

SURRENDER PRINCIPLE #3

I can always let go and
give my problems to God.

Fear tries to convince us that we don't have options, but we do! Rather than wring our hands when something comes up that we can't stop, fix, or put back on the tracks, we always have the option to take our problem to God. The inspiration for this surrender principle is 1 Peter 5:7, which says to give all of your worries and cares to God because He cares about you.

God cares about you and what you're going through! He knows that fear is a liar and has tried to convince you that you're all alone, but you are not! God not only loves you, but He cares about even the smallest details of your life.

Is there a place where you can apply this surrender principle to your life today?

Letting go of fear is hard, but it's so worth it! God doesn't want you to live in fear because, by His power, you are equipped and empowered to live by faith. Imagine what your life could look like if you let go of your fears today. If letting go of your fears feels impossible, ask God for help. He won't let you down!

Prayer

God, thank You for providing the power that takes down my stronghold of fear. Thank You for Jesus' example as well as His willingness to sacrifice His life so that I can experience life and victory in You. Amen.

Day 4: Letting Go of Others

As I'm writing this, two of my three daughters are living in areas of the world that are unfamiliar to me. My oldest daughter, Kate, graduated from the United States Military Academy and serves as a captain in the US Army. She's currently on deployment in Qatar, a country in the Middle East. As far as location goes, that's all I know other than her APO address where I send care packages to her periodically. This summer, my youngest daughter, Abbie, lives in Florida and serves with CRU during a summer evangelism missions experience while working at a theme park. Earlier today I found out that she's been living in Kissimmee, Florida, for the past eight weeks, though I've been telling everyone that she lived in Orlando. My bad! My middle daughter, Sami, lives right around the corner from me. I pick her up for church each week, so I know exactly where she lives.

You might feel like my lack of knowledge about my daughters puts me in the running for the Bad Mom of the Year award, but I like to call my comfort with this lack of information a huge sign of progress.

Daily Surrender Prayer:

God, I choose to surrender

———————

———————

———————

to You today.

Once upon a time, I was a helicopter mom. A low-flying, tight-hovering mom who believed that the more I directed my children's lives through nagging, constant checking, providing excess feedback, or what I call bubble-wrapping, the better chance they had at being successful and happy. After some intense therapy a decade ago, I can now admit I also believed that if my kids were successful, then people would say that I was a good mom.

One of the reasons I realized I needed counseling was that I was setting myself up to be god in my children's lives. Not the Almighty God, but a flawed, fearful, demi-god who wanted my kids to turn out in my own image of who I thought that they should be. My therapist challenged me with a question that still influences my parenting of my adult daughters as well as all of my relationships: *am I willing to let this person discover his or her need for God?*

This question forced me to step back and decide if I was willing to let loved ones determine their own path in life and be responsible not only for their decisions but also the consequences of their decisions. I also had to accept that some of the paths a loved one might choose could break my heart, perhaps even meaning that I would have to set firm boundaries that would prevent them from being a part of my life while the destructive behavior continued. The question I had to ask myself is, Am I *willing to step aside and allow this person to walk a road of his or her choosing, trusting that God will meet him or her whenever he or she was willing along the way?*

Today we're going to explore what it looks like to let go of trying to control others, as well as the consequences of *not* letting go and letting God work in their lives.

Think about someone in your life right now you love who has been making unhealthy decisions. How would you answer this question: *Am I willing to let this person discover his or her need for God?* **Explain your response.**

If you aren't ready to answer yes to that question, it's okay. It's not easy trying to live in the tension between helping and realizing our helping is actually hurting others. So, as you embark upon today's study, remember that prayer, discernment, and wise counsel are the best ways to sort through any control-loving behaviors that you may need to address. Most of all, don't let any self-condemnation or criticism get in the way of whatever God wants you to see today.

There's a fascinating story in the Old Testament about what happens to us when we assume responsibility for other people's problems. After the Israelites enter the Promised Land (Canaan), God instructs their new leader, Joshua, to conquer the land by fighting the thirty-one kings and kingdoms of Canaan. There is an incident that happens during Joshua's military campaign where a group of people living in the land decided to use deception to trick Joshua into fixing their problem.

Read Joshua 9:3-15, and respond to the following:

1. Circle the elements of the Gibeonites' deception:

   Dried fruit   ~~Patched sandals~~   ~~Old wineskins~~

   ~~Moldy bread~~   Old newspapers   ~~Old clothes~~

2. In verse 6, the Gibeonites ask the Israelites to make a
   treaty with them.

3. True or False: When questioned about where they lived, the Gibeonites said that they traveled from nearby (v. 6).

4. Summarize what verse 14 says about how the Israelites responded to the Gibeonites' story.

   They sampled the provisions but did not inquire of the Lord

This story highlights two human dynamics happening at the same time. First, the Gibeonites were afraid because they'd heard about the Israelites' victories against the cities of Jericho and Ai. They didn't want to face that same fate, so in their desperation to be saved, they made up a story to "sell" to the Israelites.

The second dynamic is that Joshua and the Israelites knew God's instruction not to enter into a treaty agreement with anyone living in the land of Canaan (Exodus 23:32; 34:12). However, Joshua ignores God's instructions in favor of believing the Gibeonites' story. Notice the words of Joshua 9:14: "The Israelites sampled their provisions but did not inquire of the Lord."

As we think about our interactions with others, we must remember that God is working behind the scenes in their lives just as much as He is working in ours. God allows wilderness seasons in others' lives just the same as in ours. Not everyone is open or interested in allowing God to change or transform their lives. For some of us, our only goal during wilderness seasons is finding the fastest path to an escape. This means that if we're not careful, we might be fooled into being an accomplice to aiding someone in avoiding whatever it is that God might want to teach them in that season.

Notice how I'm not saying that people are bad for some of the ways that they try to save themselves by using others. Like the Gibeonites, desperate people will sometimes do desperate things, such as lie, create stories that make others feel sorry for them, or even make promises to change even though they aren't willing to surrender their unhealthy habits or behaviors.

Can you recall a time in your life when someone told you a story or played on your emotions in hopes of getting you to bail them out? If so, write about it briefly:

Rachel
Ray

Have there been times when you have wound up rescuing people who should be responsible for their actions or behaviors? If so, write about it briefly:

In your experience, what has been the personal cost of trying to fix someone else's life? How does it impact your own well-being?

strains
emotional
& physical

Why do you think that you have been willing to pay the cost? How has it impacted the life of the other person?

heart
break

It's a good thing to want to meet the needs of others. However, Joshua's mistake in not consulting with God reminds us that there are times when we must carefully discern whether God is calling us to help, or if we need to let go and trust that God is trying to help our loved one in a different and deeper way.

When my girls were in school, I had a rule that I would only drop off forgotten homework or a lunch once during the school year. I wanted my girls to learn how to take responsibility for themselves; so at the beginning of each school year, we talked about why this rule would ultimately be for their good.

During the spring of my youngest daughter's junior year, she called me from school in tears. Unfortunately, she'd already used her "free pass" day earlier that year. She had left her application for the National Honor Society on the front table at home. The paperwork was due thirty minutes after the end of the school day.

As we talked, my mother's heart screamed, "You can fix this for her!" but I still felt conflicted. Should I break the rules just this once and run home to get the application, or do we accept what will happen if she doesn't get in? In my mind, acceptance into the National Honor Society improved her chances for a full academic scholarship. This was important because our family situation would make it difficult for us to support her financially.

As hard as it was, I explained that I couldn't rescue her during the school day because the greater value of personal responsibility had to win out. My teary girl wasn't happy, but she understood. It was a really hard conversation! While she didn't get into the National Honor Society, she did end up with a four-year academic scholarship because God provided another way. Most of all, we both learned that we need to trust God in being accountable for our actions when we mess up.

Let's get back to Joshua and the Gibeonites. The end of their story is a little more complicated. Eventually, the Israelites discovered that they have been fooled. Joshua and the leaders confront the Gibeonites, but since they've made a treaty, they are now on the hook for taking care of people whom God warned them against taking responsibility for.

Read Joshua 9:20-24 and complete the following:

The Israelites wouldn't ___*kill*___ the Gibeonites but would let them ___*live*___. (v. 20)

Though the Gibeonites would live, they would be cursed and would serve as ___*wood cutters*___ and ___*water carriers*___. (v. 21)

The Gibeonites admitted their deception because they ___*feared*___ for their lives. (v. 24)

Joshua and the Israelites would be responsible for the Gibeonite people. This new burden of responsibility was an added weight that God never intended for them to carry. The same goes for us. When we try to fix others' lives, we might be successful in certain situations, but we end up carrying the weight of responsibility for what someone should shoulder on his or her own.

If this deeply tender and sensitive topic is hitting home for you, I strongly encourage you to seek out the counsel of a trusted, wise Christian friend or pastor. It's a hard and heartbreaking situation when the people you love or care about are making irresponsible, immature, or dangerous decisions in their lives. However, we must ask ourselves if we're reacting with control-loving behaviors in order to prevent them from feeling the fallout of their choices.

Yesterday you looked up Jeremiah 29:11, which is a verse about God's plans for us. Did you realize that Jeremiah 29:11 is just as true for others as it is for you?

In the blanks below, write in the name of the person whom you've been trying to get back on track or attempting to rescue, even though he or she should be responsible for his or her own life.

*"For I know the plans I have for _____," declares the L*ORD*, "plans to prosper _____ and not to harm _____, plans to give _____ hope and a future."*

(Jeremiah 29:11)

As you see the person's name in those blanks, what is the message that God might be sending you?

While God cannot force someone to surrender his or her life to Him, He can restore and redeem anyone who surrenders to Him. Our role is to make sure that we believe God can do it and to trust Him.

Prayer

God, I can't control others, but I can control how much I am willing to allow You to work in my life. Today, I surrender my desire to fix others or rescue them from whatever You're doing in their lives. This isn't easy to do, but I trust that You will give me the courage and strength to do it. In Jesus' name. Amen.

Day 5: Practical Tools and Techniques for Letting Go

Today we'll end our week with a short and sweet lesson that offers some helpful next steps that can aid you in letting go of trying to fix or rescue others in favor of allowing the people in your life to discover their own need for God. Let's dive in!

1. Validate and wait.

When you get a phone call from someone in your life who is asking you to bail them out of a difficult situation they've created for themselves, this is a tool to help you show compassion in the moment without taking impulsive action.

First: Validate the person's stress, fear, or even panic by patiently listening to his or her story.

Avoid giving advice, because that's often like turning the doorknob on the temptation to rescue. You can say things like, "I'm so sorry to hear this," or "Gosh, that sounds like it is really hard for you to deal with."

Second: Give God space to work.

Once the person has shared his or her entire story, he or she may be waiting for you to give advice to fix that struggle or make an offer to step in and help. However, the best thing that you can do is give God space to work in the person's life by saying, "Oh, I am so glad that you've shared all of this with me. This is going to be a pretty tough problem for you to deal with, but I know that you can do it. I'm going to take some time to pray for you and ask God to give me some encouragement to share with you." You might even offer to pray with the person right then.

You may need to repeat this step if the person calls you again the next day. You do not need to make any offers to help until you've prayed and asked other trusted voices what you should do.

2. Keep your eyes on your own Hula-Hoop.

In Matthew 7:3, Jesus says, "Why do you look at the speck of sawdust in your brother's eye and pay no attention to the plank in your own eye?" When I say, "keep your eyes on your own Hula-Hoop," what I mean is "Keep your eyes on your own issues."

We tend to see other people's problems quicker than we acknowledge our own. In my experience, that plank in my eye that Jesus talks about blinds me to the impact of my own sin on the lives of others. This is why I have to engage in daily Bible study, prayer, and spiritual friendships. This is how God illuminates the dark, sinful, flawed places of my heart. Frankly, that awareness of what I need to work on is so helpful in preventing me from feeling like I should fix others first.

The bottom line is that we can invite God to work on us. We're not responsible for fixing anyone else.

3. Join the "Keep It Shut" Club.

This term is from my friend and popular author Jill Savage. As the mother of five adult children and several precious grandchildren, she talks about being a member of the "Keep It Shut" Club in her book *Empty Nest, Full Life*.

There are a lot of decisions that people around us will make. Whether it's about their clothing choices, hairstyles, tattoos or piercings; where they spend Christmas; their decorating style; or the church they attend, we're never going to agree with all of their choices. But it's also not our place to make them conform to our opinion of how they should live.

So what *should* you do?

- Keep your opinions to yourself. As Jill says, "Certainly there is a time to remind them of their heritage or upbringing, but that card needs to be used sparingly...so it's more effective."[9]
- Affirm, don't argue. The people in our lives need us to be more proactive in expressing positive words because we're often too quick to point out what they're doing wrong or need to change. I love how Jill expresses this: "The truth is, our affirmations will produce better results in their life and do far more to help them make the changes they need to make."[10]
- Talk up, not out. In the face of difficult relational dynamics, pray for these people rather than talk to them. While Jill addresses parenting issues, her following observation applies to all of our relationships: "God is far more powerful than you or me.... Your influence in prayer is much stronger than your influence in words."[11]
- If you do have to say something, follow the classic counsel: "Say what you mean, mean what you say, but don't say it meanly."

Which one of today's practical tools is most helpful for where you're struggling to let go?

Take a moment and imagine how that relationship might change or improve if you activated that tool. What improvements would you hope might take place?

Today's tools for letting go can be used for more than just your personal situation. These tools can benefit you at work, and you can teach them to anyone you might influence, such as your kids, spouse, or friends. My prayer is that they will make a very practical difference in your life.

Prayer

God, I can't control others, but I can control how much I am willing to allow You to work in my life. Today, I surrender my desire to fix others or rescue them from whatever You're doing in their lives. This isn't easy to do, but I trust that You will give me the courage and strength to do it. In Jesus' name. Amen.

Week 3 Video Viewer Guide

Numbers 20:5, 8, 10-12

We've got to know God's _~~faith~~ truth_ so that we can identify the _~~feelings~~ lies_

Satan is a great liar.

Matthew 4:5-6 *Satan presents the 2nd temptation to Jesus → misquotes Psalm 21*

Matthew 4:7

Trust God's _timeline_. *perseverance ↓ hope*

Romans 5:3-5

Surrender Principle #3

I can always _let go_ and give my problems to God.

1 Peter 5:7 *Cast all your anxieties on him because he cares for you!!*

Week 4

Letting Go of Expectations

(Matthew 4:8-11)

Memory Verse

What good is it for someone to gain the whole world, yet forfeit their soul?
(Mark 8:36)

As of May 2019, Cristiano Ronaldo had 122 million subscribers on his Facebook page. A world-renowned soccer player in his thirties, Ronaldo is the most followed person on Facebook. Just for kicks, I clicked his page to see the last post that he shared with his audience. Here's the post at the top of his page on the day that I'm writing this: "No doubts in your mind, no dandruff on your head."[1]

I'm not even kidding.

That social media post was actually sponsored by a men's shampoo company, but it still made me laugh. It also reminded me that Ronaldo had the power to influence and even get people to act on his words. In our world, influence is a currency that can buy others' attention, time, and loyalty. It's one thing to post a harmless shampoo ad, but we also know that there are others with dark and harmful agendas trying to gain influence as well.

Unlike any other time in human history, we have the ability to connect with an unlimited number of people. The good news is that we can leverage those avenues for connection to reach people to share the gospel. I love it when well-known speakers and authors use daily email technology, social media posts, simulcasts, and webinars to reach thousands of people around the world at one time. And yes, there's a dark downside because today's technology also creates may avenues for evil to influence people away from God. How should we, as believers, balance the basic human need to stand up and make a difference against our desperation to have the world revolve around us?

There's an important reason we want to address this question: I believe that God has more for you and that God has put more into you. Whatever trial or wilderness experience you're facing may provide unique opportunities for you to serve others in the future. It may be encouraging another hurting woman over a cup of coffee, starting a blog, or standing on a stage. It doesn't matter what you do, just do whatever God leads in your life. No matter who you are, I believe that God has created you to make a difference in our world. You may have the opportunity to have tremendous influence in your community or region, our country, or the world. No matter your reach, my desire is for you to be confident and not worry about the criticism of other Christians. I also pray that you stand in that place of purpose with the intention to give all glory to God rather than keep one ray of the spotlight for yourself.

Give all glory to God

Any one of us can fall into the trap of self-promotion or pride, whether it's wanting to be praised for leading a particular ministry, using a gift that's publicly recognized such as teaching or singing, or "strutting" because we hold a particular organizational position or job title. We're all susceptible to using for our own gain what others should see as God's glory.

This week, Jesus faces Satan's third temptation. The question in this temptation is, *What will you give up in order to be on top*? As we consider Satan's temptation and Jesus' response, our goal is to let go of trying to wrap our lives around our expectations of getting what we want and discover that God is and will always be all that we need.

Day 1: It's Not about You

3rd temptation. What will I give up to be on top.

Daily Surrender Prayer:

God, I choose to surrender

<u>my family</u>

to You today.

Have you ever heard the phrase "sell your soul to the devil" or "make a deal with the devil"? This idiom has been the creative seed for books, poems, plays, and music for centuries. Whether told with a backdrop of battling fiddles in the classic song "The Devil Went Down to Georgia" or in animated form on *The Simpsons*, the provocative notion that a human would sell his or her soul to Satan in exchange for something or someone endures in our world today.

Perhaps this seems like a far-fetched idea. We find it difficult to fathom that we'd ever let Satan have a bite of our sandwich, must less our souls. But what may resonate more with us is the desperation to protect what we love, fix what's broken, or get everyone and everything back on track. And this desperation may blind us at times from seeing that we've put ourselves or our desires at the top of our priorities list.

The first line in Rick Warren's book *The Purpose Driven Life: What on Earth Am I Here For* is "It's not about you."[2] Though we might say that we know the rest of the world isn't here to make us happy or give us what we want, sometimes our expectations about how life should turn out or people should behave reveal otherwise.

Extra Insight

"All high places are slippery places."[3]

Read Matthew 4:8-9, and answer the following:

What did Satan show Jesus?

all the kingdoms of the world

What did Satan tell Jesus that he could do for Him?

he would give it all to him

What would Jesus have to do in order to receive it?

bowel to him

Even though Jesus rejected the temptation to satisfy His physical needs or force God to rescue Him, the devil tempted Jesus by offering Him the world without death and suffering if Jesus would kneel down and worship him. One scholar offers a profound insight about the motivation of Satan's temptation: "This is a revealing insight into Satan's heart; worship and recognition are far more precious to him than the possession of the kingdoms of the world and their glory."[4] It's in this temptation that we see the ambition of the one the Scriptures describe as "the angel of light" (2 Corinthians 11:14-15)—the one who pretends to be from God and deceives those who follow God.

worship + recognition

The prophet Isaiah wrote about the "morning star," which scholars have interpreted to be a reference to a political leader as well as to Satan, who fell from heaven.

placing himself above God

Read Isaiah 14:12-15. Complete the statements about the morning star:

1. **His intention was to ascend to the** <u>heavens</u> **(v. 13).**

2. **He planned to raise his throne above the** <u>stars</u> **of God (v. 13).**

3. **He proposes to make himself like the** <u>Most High</u> **_____ (v. 14).**

+ ascend above the tops of the clouds

4. **Ultimately, he will be brought down to the depths of the** <u>realm of the</u> **(v. 15).**

dead to the depths of the pit

While an unbelieving world denies Jesus' divinity, Satan never doubts. He knows that Jesus is who He says He is. Now, that should tell us something, right? But that didn't stop Satan from trying to entice Jesus to trade his heavenly position in favor of immediate power and influence.

Some have questioned whether or not Satan has the power to even offer Jesus all the kingdoms of the world. On several occasions, Jesus refers to Satan as the "ruler of the world" or "prince of this world," depending on the translation (see John 12:31; 14:30; 16:11). Though Satan does have great power, he is still subject to God's sovereignty (see Hebrews 12:14 and Job 1–2, for example). While Satan works to deceive, distract, and discourage, God makes it clear that he will be punished for the harm he has inflicted on humanity and God's beloved children (see Isaiah 14:15 and Revelation 20:7-15).

John 12:31 "The prince of this world will be driven out"

16:11 So the prince of this world now stands condemned

Whether Satan tempted Jesus with worldly ambition because of his own ambition or his awareness of the human tendency to seek power and control, the temptation resonates with our humanity. If we look again to the Israelites in the wilderness, Moses demonstrates how to hold a position of authority while giving God the top spot in his life.

Read Numbers 12:3. What quality did Moses possess?

humility

In his well-known definition of humility, Rick Warren writes: "Humility isn't thinking less of yourself; it is thinking of yourself less."[5] Humility is what we learn when we see our shortcomings and our strengths through God's eyes. I love how Warren describes it this way: "Humility isn't denying your strengths; humility is being honest about your weaknesses. The more humble you are, the more God's grace you get. The more God's grace you get, the more power you have."[6]

How would you define *humility* in your own words?

Putting God 1st + others before myself   *being honest about our weaknesses*

Read Proverbs 11:2 and 1 Peter 5:5 in the margin. How do these verses challenge our control-loving behaviors?

humility - listen more → learn more   *humility provides wisdom. pride disgrace*

Humility leads to God's favor

How does humility open the door for God to bless us?

Allows us to be in service to God.

like Moses we find God's favor

Moses knew that being the leader of the Israelites wasn't about him. He knew that his job was to point people toward God. How did he come to be so humble and dependent upon God?

Moses was supernaturally saved at a time when Pharaoh ordered the deaths of infant Hebrew boys. He ended up growing up in Pharaoh's household and was well educated and became a man of great speech and action (Acts 7:22). Then he messed up. When he was forty, he killed an Egyptian and hid the body. He ran away and ended up working for a man named Jethro. While he had once lived in Pharaoh's household, Moses spent forty years in the wilderness as a shepherd.

Moses' life was a mix of big highs and lows before God called him to lead the Israelites. Perhaps his humility came because he saw God's hand moving in the background of his life. Moses used his strengths to lead; and although he got upset and frustrated at times, he lived to lead people to God.

Humility is not thinking less of yourself it's thing of yourself less

When pride comes, then comes disgrace, but with humility comes wisdom.
(Proverbs 11:2)

All of you, clothe yourselves with humility toward one another, because, "God opposes the proud but shows favor to the humble."
(1 Peter 5:5)

where do you see God's hand in background of your life? Does it humble you?

Who are some of your favorite humble people? What do you admire about them?

Lynn => quiet, composed
Amanda => sees other's viewpoints
my husband - shows such grace in adversity

What would it look like for you to intentionally practice humility in your life?

Kinder
Think of others more than me

What are the strengths that you should be using for the glory of God?

helping others
willingness to work

Where do you need to be more authentic about your struggles and God's grace in your life?

I need to make time for you alone, Lord

Memory Verse Reflection

Refer to Mark 8:36 and fill in the blanks:

What good is it for someone to _____*gain*_____ the whole _____*world*_____, yet forfeit their _____*soul*_____?

(Mark 8:36)

Based on what you've studied today, what does this verse mean to you?

what if you have everything oro lots of money, things etc etc but no relationship c God

In my life, humility means I know that God has gifted me, and as well He has granted me precious second chances after many mistakes and failures. Staying humble means I expose myself to the truth of God's Word to challenge those "It's all about you" whispers as well as surround myself with trusted voices who make it safe for me to work through the tough challenges and temptations in my life. Finally, I get to practice humility by sharing the hard parts of my life with others and talking about how God's grace upon grace blesses me in those heartbreaking places. This is how I work on being humble and giving glory to God.

Prayer

God, I will worship You alone. There are so many temptations and distractions competing for my focus, but I will keep my focus on remembering who You are and what You have done—not only in my life but also from the beginning of time. I offer myself to live for Your glory. In Jesus' name. Amen.

Day 2: Tough Trials Do End!

Daily Surrender Prayer:

God, I choose to surrender ~~my hurts/ frustrations~~ *to You today.*

One year I attended a favorite women's ministry event at a time when our family crisis of addiction was compounded by the death of a beloved family member. For a second, I thought about not going, but I knew that I needed a few days away so that I could rest and be refreshed in order step back into facing my wilderness circumstances.

That year the speaker of the conference shared an update on her family. I'd been praying for her family and following her social media posts for the previous year. Her large ministry platform didn't insulate her from life's devastating heartaches.

In a precious moment on the final night of the event, she shared a tender and inspiring story of restoration. Tears flowed as she shared the bumpy and often brutal road back from brokenness and pain. My heart overflowed with joy for her and her family. Yet I couldn't hush the tiny, teary whisper in the back of my mind that cried out to God: "Why couldn't that have happened for me, God?"

If you're in the middle of a trial or a wilderness season, it might seem like it will last forever. But it won't. While there are some illnesses that won't be healed, some relationships that won't be mended, and some financial setbacks that never make a comeback, the actual *crisis* itself won't last forever. Everything happening today in your life will eventually be a memory.

God will get me through

There's something simple that I say to myself whenever I'm facing a hard or heartbreaking moment: "You're going to be okay. God will get you through this." This brings me hope and gives me perspective on whatever I'm facing at the moment, and I hope it brings hope to you too.

Jesus said to him, "Away from me, Satan! For it is written: 'Worship the Lord your God, and serve him only.'"

(Matthew 4:10)

Read Matthew 4:10 in the margin. What's the first thing Jesus says to Satan?

Away from me!!

Submit yourselves, then, to God. Resist the devil, and he will flee from you.

(James 4:7)

Read James 4:7 in the margin. How can we resist the devil?

Submit myself to God.

Sometimes we've just got to resist! That might mean turning from temptation or telling Satan to be gone in Jesus' name! We can't control him, but we can let him know that we're going to stand in God's power against his attempts to mess up our lives.

In the face of each temptation, Jesus began each of His replies to Satan with the same preface. "For it is _written_ **."**
(Refer again to Matthew 4:10.)

We can never forget that temptation is real, so we need the truth and power of God's Word to fight Satan's attempts to destroy our lives and our futures. We can't play with lesser strategies such as willpower because Satan's power will overwhelm our willpower every time. If Jesus used Scripture to battle Satan, then we should too!

Jesus' response to Satan in Matthew 4:10 comes from Deuteronomy 6:13. Read the verse below, and underline the portions that Jesus used in his response to Satan.

Fear the LORD your God, serve him only and take your oaths in his name.

(Deuteronomy 6:13)

Once again Jesus refers to a passage of Scripture from the Israelites' years of wandering in the desert. Unlike the other two Deuteronomy passages that speak of God's provision in hard times, this passage calls God's people to maintain clarity on worshiping God when times are more prosperous and people come into more possessions. *✳ even in prosperity worship*

In Deuteronomy 6, Moses teaches the people about how to handle the blessings of the Promised Land. After forty years of wandering in the wilderness, the Israelites not only would experience a new place to call home but they also would face temptation, as conquering the new land would bring in new voices, influences, distractions, and the lure of possessions. Deuteronomy 6:13 is just one of many warnings Moses gave to the people about not forgetting God. He knew that they were at risk of forgetting all about how God led them through those years through a cloud during the day and a pillar of fire at night. God didn't want them to leave His story out of their wilderness history.

How do the warnings in the following verses translate to what you might be facing in your life today?

Only be careful, and watch yourselves closely so that you do not forget the things your eyes have seen or let them fade from your heart as long

Extra Insight

"If Jesus had worshiped Satan in order to gain worldly power, it would have indicated that he valued creation more than the Creator and the kingdoms of earth more than the kingdom of God."[7]

as you live. Teach them to your children and to their children after them.

(Deuteronomy 4:9)

Be careful not to forget the covenant of them LORD *your God that he made with you; do not make for yourselves an idol in the form of anything the* LORD *your God has forbidden.*

(Deuteronomy 4:23)

> Carry on the story of God.
> Teach your children well
> Never forget even the trials
>   are lessons. Be careful regarding
> my idols

I love that both verses begin with "be careful." This translates to "be intentional about remembering." Since we can be forgetful when life is easy, remembering on a regular basis keeps us connected to where we've come from and what God has brought us through.

do I only turn to God in need

Look up the following verses and summarize these "remembering" lessons:

Numbers 15:40

The tassels will help you remember to obey the commandments + be loyal to your God

what can you use to remember?

Psalm 77:11
**
memories of Gods miracles sustained the Israelites in hard time

Ecclesiastes 12:1
don't let the excitement of youth forget your creator - (don't wait til you are old to appreciate his wonder

Hebrews 8:12
and I will forget their wickedness + never remember their sin

Grace

There's an uncomfortable paradox that I cannot ignore about my spiritual life: when life is hard, that's when it's easier for me to stay close to God; but when life is easy, that's when I struggle to stay close to God.

When life is easy, we may not always ask the hard questions or expect God to show up in big ways in our lives. When life is easy, more often than not, we feel like we've got things under control.

Oddly enough, even though the wilderness is a wild, unpredictable, and painful place, it's always the season of life when I see God do the amazing (like show up and help me write this study!). A few times, I've wondered whether or not the wilderness season of life is a better place for me to be. Comfort feels good, but it can frustrate our attempts to focus on faith.

How do you struggle to stay faithful when life seems to be under control?

I take things for granted
I don't take the time to pray,
I always remember when bad
things happen

Read Psalm 100 aloud. Underline the reasons why we should worship God, and circle what we should do as acts of worship.

¹Shout for joy to the LORD, all the earth.
    ²Worship the LORD with gladness;
    come before him with joyful songs.
³Know that the LORD is God.
    It is he who made us, and we are his;
    we are his people, the sheep of his pasture.

⁴Enter his gates with thanksgiving
    and his courts with praise;
    give thanks to him and praise his name.
⁵For the LORD is good and his love endures forever;
    his faithfulness continues through all generations.
                    (Psalm 100:1-5)

Reading Psalm 100 flows nicely into the introduction of this week's surrender principle, which captures the cause and effect of what happens when we focus on God versus when we focus on trying to fix our circumstances.

SURRENDER PRINCIPLE #4

Trusting God's promises will bless me,
but pushing my plans will stress me.

Reflection Exercise

In the space below or on a separate sheet of paper, write a letter to God about why it is so important for you to keep Him, rather than your own needs and desires, as the central focus of your life.

Dear God,

I get so distracted + forget that all my blessings + gifts come from you. You love me no matter what I do + forget all my terrible words + thoughts + deeds!!

Perhaps today's study has changed your plans for the day. Maybe you had been thinking and rethinking about how to tackle a problem that has been stressing you out, and the solution you settled on was stressing you out as well. As you read today's prayer, give yourself time to remember what God has already done for you. When you celebrate God's faithfulness, you'll discover that your fears will melt away.

Prayer

God, I come to You with a thankful heart. You've been so faithful to me. Thank You for ___*Paul, my children, my love*___ *and how You provided* ___*my pups*___ ___*strength + resources + problem solving*___ *for me when times were tough. Today, I choose to focus on You and not my problems. I worship You as God Almighty. I am grateful that You are in control. In Jesus' name. Amen.*

Day 3: Letting Go of Entitlement

Yesterday you read Jesus' response to Satan's offer to give Jesus all the kingdoms of the world if Jesus would bow down and worship him. Again, while most of us don't want to admit that we're competing with God for the top spot in our lives, there are many times when that's actually the case.

Today we're going to look at how our perception of how things should be often gets in our way of trusting God's heart when it comes to what's happening in our lives.

I've heard it said that expectations are the path to resentment. When we hold expectations, we often make assumptions about what we should receive

Daily Surrender Prayer:

God, I choose to surrender ___*the*___ ___*job*___ ___ *to You today.*

or what we shouldn't have to experience. Yet when trials or wilderness seasons come, we're caught off guard, thinking, *Life wasn't supposed to happen this way!*

In those moments, have you ever thought, I don't deserve this? It's not fair! I'm a good person, so why is this happening to me?

One of the buzzwords in our culture today is *entitlement*. Entitlement sets in when we feel we are owed or should own something. Whether it's people who expect a perfect family vacation because they paid a lot of money for it, an employee who takes extra time off without recording it because they don't like their manager, or someone who offers sharp "side eye" if someone dares to sit in their seat at church, entitlement can come in a lot of different shapes, sizes, and motivations.

Over the summer my youngest daughter worked at a well-known theme park. She expressed frustration with customers who yelled and even bullied employees when a ketchup container was empty or a sandwich was missing bacon. She remarked that customers justified their rude behavior with the common explanation, "I paid a lot of money to come here." In their minds, paying for a high-priced vacation meant that they deserved their expectations to be met. This is an example of entitled thinking.

In a spiritual sense, entitlement is one by-product of our control-loving mentality. As long as we think we have power over others and outcomes, then we believe that what we love should be protected, what is broken should be fixed, and things should get back on track if we work hard enough at it.

Today we're going to explore one of the stories that Jesus taught to an audience, particularly a group of religious leaders who were trapped in an entitlement mentality. Jesus wanted the crowd to discover that God's love, hope, and grace don't belong only to those who think that they deserve it.

Read Luke 15:11-24, and answer T or F:

____ T ____ 1. The father divided his estate after his younger son requested his inheritance.

____ F ____ 2. The younger son took his money and built a new home next door.

____ T ____ 3. After spending all of his inheritance, the younger son ended up feeding pigs.

____ F ____ 4. At some point, the younger son made more money and went back to wild living.

____ T ____ 5. Eventually, the younger son came to his senses and traveled back home.

[handwritten margin note: Expectations = path to resentment]

_F_ 6. The father wasn't excited to see his younger son return home again.

_T_ 7. The younger son confessed his sin, and the father welcomed him back home.

You may be familiar with the story of the prodigal, or lost, son, in which Jesus paints a story of forgiveness and grace. The people listening in the crowd would have been angry at the young man who carelessly took half of his father's estate while his father was still living and then wasted the fruits of his father's labor on wild living. Later, after the young man comes to his senses and comes home, not only does the father celebrate his son's return, but he fully restores the son's place in the family.

In this story, there are many layers that all reflect the power of God's love and grace for those who are lost. Yet there's a second part to this story that applies to what we're talking about today. Instead of stopping at the happy ending, Jesus continued.

Read Luke 15:25-30. What was the older brother doing when he found out that his younger brother finally returned home?

working in the fields

Why was the older brother so angry?

he felt entitled to the father's estate

The older brother was in the field working. While the parable of the lost son is a story, the audience would have imagined that the older brother was the good son who didn't ask for his inheritance. Even after his younger brother ran off, breaking his father's heart and causing shame and scandal to their family's reputation, the older brother kept going out into the fields to responsibly carry on.

So why did he get so angry? The answer is found in his response to the father: "Look! All these years I've been slaving for you and never disobeyed your orders. Yet you never gave me even a young goat so I could celebrate with my friends" (v. 29). The older son was angry because his irresponsible brother wasted half the family's estate, broke all of the rules, and still received grace.

Does it make you mad when people don't get what they deserve? Explain your response.

Sometimes it doesn't seem fair that others get more

Read Luke 15:31-32. How does the father respond to his angry older son?

He tells the older son that we must rejoice because he has found his way home. The way we will need to find our way back to God

Rather than yelling at his older son for being mean and rude, the father answers with compassion, acknowledging the elder son's faithfulness and future blessing. While the older brother believes that he deserves a little something extra for not getting off track, the father's love for both of his sons—the rebellious and the steady—remains the same.

I grew up with an elder brother mentality. I followed the rules and looked down on those who didn't. I figured that God liked me a little bit more because I was good. During my college years, I ran the road of the prodigal for a short period of time. It was then that I discovered the power of grace! I'd messed up so badly that only God could redeem my mistakes. Yet in that low point in my life, I was so grateful that I didn't have to measure up for God to love or forgive me. I discovered that there was nothing I could do to make God love me more and nothing I could do to make God love me less. Grace is grace for everyone, whether you've never had a wild day in your life or you've just made the worst mistake of your life. Grace is for everyone at all times. Praise God!

"Elder brother" people reject needing a savior because they don't realize that they need saving. Elder brother types think that following rules will get them whatever they want or need. But the truth is, rule following is hollow apart from a relationship with God based on love.

Pastor and author Tim Keller offers this insight about the older son: "He cares about the father's things; he doesn't care about the father's heart."[8] Following God in order to get something from God is a control mentality that robs us of peace and joy. Keller's words are an important temperature check for us: Are we following God because we love Him, or are we using God to get what we want?

Can you think of some examples of when you might display the actions or attitudes of the elder brother?

At work or it's in jealousy or seeing those succeed who have been so mean

The elder brother is a symbol for those who believe that God owes us some kind of *quid pro quo*—if we follow God's rules, then we deserve a good life. It's a subtle form of trying to motivate or control God to give us what we want. The older brother demonstrates that following the rules doesn't mean that our heart is in the right place. Jesus addresses this very thing with a bold challenge to the religious leaders of His time.

Read Luke 11:42. How did the Pharisees' behavior reflect a similar attitude as that of the elder brother?

Entitlement

As I reflect on the wilderness seasons in my life, some of the lessons that I've learned directly address the entitlement mindset that leads me to believe I should have what I want when I want it. While our culture contends with racial or economic entitlement issues, there are individual entitlement attitudes as well. Since we live in a first-world environment, sometimes we forget that what we've achieved, possess, or own didn't come from our own hands but was given to us by God's hand.

Entitlement is the combination of three self-seeking behaviors. It takes a step of humility for us to consider where entitlement attitudes might be hidden in our hearts and minds, and I invite you to take this step with me.

Pride
(I'm more important than you are)
+
Materialism
(Having and owning is a top priority)
+
Ungratefulness
(Why don't I have more?)

= Entitlement (I'm owed or I should own)

Where do you see entitlement in our families, workplaces, or American culture?

That we deserve $, material things, recognition etc...

Where do you see entitlement lurking around your life, particularly your spiritual life with God?

Sometimes I forget that my gifts professionally came from you Lord. You helped/made me get them

How does entitlement keep us from fully experiencing God's grace or completely trusting God?

It can make us forget it's not about me!!

If the recipe for entitlement is pride, materialism, and ungratefulness, then the letting go of entitlement means cultivating the opposite in our lives. Each of the words in the following pairs of opposites is both a principle and a practice, meaning that we only experience the fullness of it as we engage in it. When you practice these anti-entitlement qualities, you'll realize that your focus will move from the posture of believing that you deserve to have what you want, to opehandedly allowing God to decide what you will or will not receive.

Match the opposites by drawing a line from one column to the other.

Pride   Generosity

Ungratefulness   Humility

Materialism   Thankfulness

Read Philippians 2:3-4 in the margin. What are some practical ways to demonstrate humility?

Look toward the interests of others

Read Luke 6:38 in the margin. What is the principle of generosity in this verse?

Look more to the interests of others and it will be given to you

Read Romans 1:21 in the margin. What happens when we refuse to give thanks to God for what He has done in our lives?

thinking becomes futile + your heart is darkened

[3] Do nothing out of selfish ambition or vain conceit. Rather, in humility value others above yourselves, [4] not looking to your own interests but each of you to the interests of the others.
(Philippians 2:3-4)

"Give, and it will be given to you. A good measure, pressed down, shaken together and running over, will be poured into your lap. For with the measure you use, it will be measured to you."
(Luke 6:38)

For although they knew God, they neither glorified him as God nor gave thanks to him, but their thinking became futile and their foolish hearts were darkened.
(Romans 1:21)

Extra Insight

"An attitude of gratitude is a wonderful weapon against unbelief, disobedience, a hard heart, and a bitter spirit."[9]

Practice gratitude

Reflect on the verses you've read today on humility, generosity, and thankfulness, as well as your own current surrender situation, and consider some practical ways you can move away from entitlement.

One way I can practice humility today:

Pray fn others
Retrain my thoughts
when I am thinking selfishly

One way I can demonstrate generosity today:

Be kind to Rachel
Pray fn her

One way I can express my thankfulness to God today:

Just tell him
Obey his commands

Addressing entitlement comes with a beautiful opportunity for you! You had the chance to identify three ways to practice entitlement-busting behaviors today. My prayer is that you will lean into one of those, not because I'm asking you to, but because you want to let go of an attitude that can undermine your desire to grow in your faith.

Prayer

God, how often I forget that what I have and who I am are only because of what You've given to me! Help me to see where the roots of entitlement have woven their way into my heart and mind. Today I want to practice humility, generosity, and thankfulness so that I can keep my heart and mind on You. Give me the desire to let go and let You transform my heart. In Jesus' name. Amen.

Day 4: Letting Go of People-Pleasing

As we've been studying Satan's attempt to get Jesus to bow down in exchange for all of the kingdoms of the world, you may have thought, "Well, I don't care about having lots of things, and I don't care about being popular." But most of us *do* care that other people like us. I've met a lot of people, and I can't recall running into someone who lives to be disliked.

It's easy to silently criticize those who are vocal about their desire to be famous, friended, or followed. It's much harder to consider whether or not we say or do things in efforts to get people to like us.

Today we're talking about people-pleasing, which can be a control-loving technique to get people to like us so that we can get something from them that we want—whether we want to feel like we belong, gain influence, or get others to fix a problem for us.

There's a powerful story in Exodus about Moses' brother, Aaron, who ended up engaging in some people-pleasing while Moses was away talking with God. While Aaron didn't force the people to sin, his actions didn't help people to move toward God; and there were some awful consequences as a result.

Read Exodus 32:1, and answer the following questions.

Why were the people concerned?

that Moses had not returned in a timely way + they needed a "God" to lead them

What did they want Aaron to do for them?

make them a God

What did they say about Moses?

he had been gone too long

Whereas Satan took Jesus to a high mountain to tempt Him to worship him, God called Moses to a high mountain to explain what it means to worship Him. Both Jesus and Moses spent forty days and forty nights in their respective situations. Unfortunately, God's people didn't handle their situation well.

I don't know why, but I chuckle every time I read the Israelites' response: "As for this fellow Moses who brought us up out of Egypt, we don't know what has happened to him" (Exodus 32:1). I know it's not funny. It's actually far from funny, because how could the people forget about the guy who stood in front of the Red Sea and parted the waters? However, while Moses was on the mountain, an "out of sight, out of mind" mentality penetrated the crowd. As the people grew restless, they resorted to what they knew, which was idol worship.

Moses had given his brother, Aaron, and another man named Hur authority in his absence (Exodus 24:14). Let's see what happened.

Read Exodus 32:2-6, and match the left column with the right column.

_D_ 1. This precious metal was used to make the idol. A. Calf

_E_ 2. He created the idol. B. Altar

_A_ 3. The idol looked like this animal. C. Festival

_F_ 4. The people referred to the animal as this. D. Gold

_B_ 5. Aaron built this in front of the idol. E. Aaron

_C_ 6. At this event, the people went wild. F. god

The people came to Aaron looking for an idol, but that's not what they needed. One scholar observes: "Israel didn't know how to live by faith and trust God regardless of who their leader was."[10]

Rather than encourage the people to trust the God who had performed many miracles in their rescue and survival, Aaron's solution was to appease the crowd by giving them what they asked for. So he took the gold jewelry, melted it down, and gave the people an idol. Essentially, he aided them in breaking God's first commandment.

While it's one thing to love an adorable cow, the Israelites got excited about the golden calf because it "fit well with both Egyptian and Canaanite practices, in which the calf was a symbol of strength and fertility."[11] God brought His people into the wilderness to get the wilderness out of the people. They'd spent generations in Egypt, so idol worship was all that they knew—and what they returned to once there was a lull in between miracles.

While we may ridicule Aaron for making a golden calf—something that we'd never worship in our culture today—perhaps we can relate to his people-pleasing behavior or the "disease to please," as some have called it. There are a few hallmarks of people-pleasing behavior, such as trying to agree with everyone, the inability to say no, a deep desire to avoid conflict, not wanting people to be upset with you, or the inability to express yourself when you're mad.[12]

Are you a people-pleaser? Circle the number on the line below to indicate where you think you are now:

1	2	3	4	5	6	7	8	9	10
Nope		Rarely		Depends		Struggle to say "no" or not cave		I rarely assert my opinions or wishes	

Answers: 1. D 2. E 3. A 4. F 5. B 6. C

Regardless of your score, who do you feel pressured to make happy?

*children   family   my boss
my sisters   my employees*

When do you feel like you can't be honest about how you're feeling?

*4 I feel like it may
threaten a relationship on my status
in life*

How can people-pleasing actually function as a form of controlling behavior?

*it's a lack of honesty but allows
you to keep people in your presence*

Has your people-pleasing behavior ever enabled another's bad/sinful choices? If so, write about it briefly:

my children

In your opinion, what is the difference between being a people-pleaser and someone who wants to show unconditional love and serve selflessly?

*Unconditional love is honest
+ pure*

I've never considered myself a people-pleaser, but there have been times in my life when I felt insecure in my job or a relationship and did what I could to gain the approval of others. During those times it seemed like saying "yes" or "I'm good" was a good way to keep the peace in a bad situation. However, the go-along-to-get-along approach, particularly between believers, undermines authentic connection and unity. We've all probably witnessed people-pleasers unintentionally supporting irresponsible choices or the bad behavior of others. Without meaning to, those people-pleasers can be accomplices to someone's self-destruction.

Although the following verse can be misused, it holds a powerful spiritual principle.

Read Ephesians 4:15 in the margin. When we speak the "truth in love," how does that transform us spiritually?

helps to build a body of believers

Unfortunately, this verse has been used to justify Christians' disgraceful comments to people who think, act, or live differently. I've seen one woman shame another woman for what she's wearing to church, only to end the conversation with, "Honey, I'm just speaking the truth in love to you." Just because we tell someone that we want to tell them the "truth in love" doesn't mean that we're actually doing it.

Read Ephesians 4:15 again. What benefit do we experience as believers when we actually tell people the truth in love?

We become the body of Christ but it's about issues that matter NOT clothing

Speak the truth in love

We often emphasize that this verse is about the people we're speaking love to, but it's just as important to remember that each time we speak the truth with the same loving attitude as Christ, we become more like Him. It follows, then, that when we speak the truth, but not in love, we're undermining our goal to be more like Christ.

How can you know that you are speaking the truth in love? What are some of the indications?

Building someone up instead of tearing down.

Just to be clear, it's vital that believers watch out for one another.

Read Galatians 6:1 in the margin. Why is it important for believers to address sin in one another's lives?

One scholar captures the essence of the "truth in love" phrase this way: "The truth must not be used as a club to bludgeon people into acceptance and obedience but must always be presented in love. The truth leads the Christian to maturity, which is defined here as growing up into Christ."[13]

On the other hand, there are times when the truth must be spoken even at the risk of the relationship, and the consequences of not speaking up cost a great deal for all involved.

While Moses is on the mountain, God tells him to return to the people because they've begun to worship an idol. Moses came down from the mountain with two tablets full of instructions from God. However, he was so angry when he saw the golden calf and the wild party before him that he threw down the tablets, breaking them into pieces. He took the calf, melted it down, mixed it with water, and made the people drink it. One commentary explains, "Drinking water containing the ground up golden calf meant that whatever was left of the calf would become nothing but human waste."[14]

Then Moses turned his attention to Aaron.

Read Exodus 32:21-25. Why did Aaron tell Moses not to be angry?

You know those people are one another and. you know what their like

How did Aaron explain the golden calf?

like no big deal

I can see Aaron shrugging his shoulders at Moses' questions and blaming the people: "Come on, Bro, you know how these people are, right?" One source said it like this: "Aaron's account minimizes his participation by leaving out much of what he did and by describing the calf a surprise."[15] It's like Aaron was saying, "Gosh, Moses, I have no idea how this happened!" even though Aaron project-managed the entire calf-casting event.

The story ends with Moses recruiting men who would identify and punish those who led the rebellion.

Read Exodus 32:35 in the margin. What happened as a result of the rebellion?

struck them c̄ a plague

And the LORD struck the people with a plague because of what they did with the calf Aaron had made.

(Exodus 32:35)

A lot of people died because they rebelled against God. However, Aaron wasn't responsible for the people's wayward hearts. Those involved in the rebellion would have found something to worship if Aaron had refused to make the golden calf—just as we do with our own wayward hearts. The important point here is that Aaron had a chance and a choice to point the people back to God, but he was too afraid to do it.

Read 1 Corinthians 8:9 in the margin. What are some ways that people-pleasing behavior can become a stumbling block to others, either preventing them from seeing the real consequences of their actions or interfering with their spiritual journey?

Be careful, however, that the exercise of your rights does not become a stumbling block to the weak.

(1 Corinthians 8:9)

Years ago I worked with someone, a friend, who didn't seem to be putting forth the best effort at work. This person was getting away with behaviors that weren't wrong or sinful, but it did create some ill will among others. There were several times when I felt prompted to speak up and address the issue but feared the loss of the friendship and the fallout. Years later, a large fallout did happen, and in time this person repented. Though God redeemed a very painful situation, I had to ask God for forgiveness because I was disobedient in being afraid of confronting a friend who probably needed the voice of truth spoken in love.

Like the stronghold of fear we explored last week, people-pleasing also can be a stronghold and a control-loving behavior; because as long as we can keep people happy with us, then we don't have to fear loss of connection, judgment, or isolation. Yet trying to control others' opinion of us undermines what God wants to do in our lives and how He wants to use us in the lives of others—sometimes to literally save lives.

While Jesus worked in public ministry, He was ridiculed, targeted, and even rejected for telling the truth. Yet He persisted because He understood the magnificent mission of His life, which was to seek and save the lost. That was worth all of the negative words and attitudes of others.

Look up the following verses and complete the lesson we learn from each verse:

Galatians 1:10
"If I were still trying to please __people__ *, I would not be a servant of Christ."*

Proverbs 29:25
"Fear of man will prove to be a __trap__ *, but whoever trusts in the* Lord *is kept safe."*

1 Thessalonians 2:4
"We are not trying to please people __but God__ *, who tests our hearts."*

What would it look like for you to let go of people-pleasing behavior, especially when your yeses or silence actually aids them in dangerous, divisive, or unhealthy behavior? Rather than trying to figure out how to stop people-pleasing, perhaps it's more productive to practice speaking the truth in love. The more that you learn how to do this, the less you'll default to people-pleasing behaviors. Here is a tool that outlines practical steps you can follow:

Power over People-Pleasing

1. **PRAY**. Ask God to reveal a situation where you've been keeping the peace by not speaking truth.

2. **PRACTICE**. What do you need to say to that person? Write on a separate sheet of paper what you need to say, remembering that Jesus calls us to speak the "truth in love." (Or perhaps you don't need to say something but to consider helping someone in some way.)

3. **PROMPTING**. Pray over your paper and tell God that you will listen for His prompting the next time you're talking with that person.

4. **PARTNER**. Let a friend know that you need to have a hard conversation with someone in your life. You don't have to share the details, but you do want someone praying about the situation with you and for you.

5. **LET GO OF THE OUTCOME.** Begin praying now that you will surrender the results of your conversation to God. Just because you share the truth in love doesn't mean that the other person will listen. Additionally, begin surrendering any rejection or negative consequences that may happen after you have the conversation. Ask God to reassure you of His unconditional love and to help you accept any potential hardship or heartache that may come from sharing the necessary truth in love.

If your mind is heavy with conviction over some unhelpful or unhealthy people-pleasing behaviors, can I encourage you to refrain from sinking into self-condemnation? You aren't alone if people-pleasing is a struggle. I encourage you to consider following the "Power over People-Pleasing" steps in an effort to live out Ephesians 4:15 and speak the truth in love. Don't let fear or even temporary fallout keep you from pursuing God's best for you *and* those you care about!

Prayer

God, it's so hard to speak the truth when I'm afraid of losing a relationship or experiencing a harsh reaction or consequence. However, I choose to hold on to Joshua 1:9 and remember that I can be strong and courageous because You will be with me in that situation. Give me the words to speak the truth in love as well as the conviction to follow through on the conversation. In Jesus' name. Amen.

Day 5: Letting Go of Stuff

In my humble opinion, there are two types of women: those who pack their purses with everything needed to survive in the jungle for a week and those who carry only a wallet and lip balm yet know where to find the nearest drug store in an emergency. Which one are you?

In my lifetime, I've been both. During previous seasons of life, particularly the seasons when I waged a long battle against what I called the anxious "what if's," I spent a lot of time buying extras that turned into excess because I didn't like the feeling of powerlessness when I didn't have what I needed.

My friend and author Kathi Lipp calls this kind of living "just in case thinking." In her book *Clutter Free*, Kathi shares her tendency to buy, keep, or pack everything she could possibly need in a situation, whether she would need it herself or could use it to help someone else. For instance, Kathi writes about having fifty plates in case she ever had a large dinner party, but she later realized she only had room for sixteen people in her home.

As Kathi reflected on her journey toward becoming clutter free, she asked herself two questions: "Why do I have to be prepared for every possibility? Why do I have to be the bottom line for everything?"[16] Her eye-opening answer to those questions is this: "Fear that I won't have enough. Fear that I will be stuck without something and not know what to do."[17]

As we're exploring this week, Satan offered Jesus the entire world if Jesus would bow down and worship him. We've looked at a variety of areas where we need to let go of entitlement, insecurity, and people-pleasing—because those things feed our pride or undermine our desire to worship God. Today we will examine another question related to the temptation to worship anything other than God: *What does it cost us when we're spending more time managing our stuff than serving Jesus?*

Let's begin with looking at a passage of Scripture in the Sermon on the Mount where Jesus calls His followers to be accountable for what they have and to know the motivations for why they have it.

Read Matthew 6:19 in the margin and answer the following questions:

Does Jesus say that it is a sin to have material possessions?

What will eventually happen to everything that we accumulate on this earth?

it will rot

"Do not store up for yourselves treasures on earth, where moths and vermin destroy, and where thieves break in and steal."
(Matthew 6:19)

Are there any material possessions that you spend a lot of time protecting, fixing up or repairing, or replenishing?

my house

my clothing

What does it feel like for you to imagine your car, your favorite clothes, your jewelry, or some other treasured possession deteriorating in a trash dump one day?

God isn't against us having material possessions. Abraham, David, and Solomon were wealthy men, and the Scriptures point out that God was the one who blessed them with great wealth. No one should criticize you for wanting or having a nice home, driving a fabulous car, or even having a yacht—feel free to invite me to sail with you! It's not about what we have; it's about why we have it and whether or not we'll allow God to use it or remove it. As one scholar writes, "It is not wrong for us to possess things, but it is wrong for things to possess us."[18]

There are a lot of reasons our things can possess us. Sometimes it's a fear of not having enough or a desire for our stuff to make us feel successful or to fill an emptiness inside us. Are any of these reasons true for you? If so, write about it briefly:

I have always wanted to feel pretty but maybe it's my heart that needs to be prettier.

Is there some possession in your life that you find yourself talking about more than God? If so, why has it become so important to you?

Years ago, a sweet friend of mine was building a new home. She was so excited, but she was aware of how quickly she could get wrapped up in thinking and planning for her new home instead of focusing on God. I'll never forget the day she asked me to hold her accountable. She said, "Look, if I ever get to the point when I'm talking about this house more than God, you've got to let me know." She was smart enough to know how quickly her heart could fall in love with something other than God.

Read Matthew 6:21 below. Draw a dollar sign over the word *treasure* and a heart over the word *heart*. Then draw an arrow between the two symbols.

$ ⟶ ♡

For where your treasure is, there your heart will be also.

In Dietrich Bonhoeffer's classic *The Cost of Discipleship*, he writes, "The life of discipleship can only be maintained so long as nothing is allowed to come between Christ and ourselves.... Worldly possessions tend to turn the hearts of the disciples away from Jesus."[19]

One of the ladies in my Bible study group owns several successful businesses, so she can buy whatever she wants. As she grew spiritually, she sensed that the care and management of her stuff was taking her away from the things that God wanted her to do. One summer she hosted a massive parking lot sale, which included hundreds of pairs of shoes and thousands of articles of clothing all on sale for $3.00 each. Whatever she didn't sell, she donated to charity. For her, letting go of her stuff was like lifting a large weight off her heart and mind.

Maybe you don't own a lot of stuff, but the same principle applies. If you're preoccupied with what you want to buy or you panic at the thought of losing a possession, it's good to ask yourself whether or not it's interfering with your heart's desire for Jesus.

It's hard to have peace when our hearts and minds are fixated on protecting our possessions, not on our relationship with God. Jesus addresses this in a story about a man who had abundance but didn't practice wisdom in how he used his abundance.

Read Luke 12:17-21 and answer the following questions:

What was the man's problem? (v. 17)

He didn't realize his gift was from God. } *too much grain*

What was his solution, and what was his plan once he accomplished his solution? (vv. 18-19)

built himself a bigger barn

Why did God call the man a fool? (vv. 20-21)

None of us wants to be a fool, right? So, how do we learn to let go of trying to get or hold on to material possessions that ultimately have no eternal value? If Jesus says that our hearts will follow our treasure, then the key is to make sure that our treasure is God; and that means we've got to have a heart that surrenders stuff. We can teach our heart to surrender our stuff by practicing giving it away.

What are some "just in case" things that you've been holding on to?

We buy too much food
Too many clothes

What do you sense God speaking to you right now about those possessions?

Time to give them away

Here's the secret about our stuff: it's not ours anyway!

One of the reasons God gave manna each day to the children of Israel in the wilderness was to teach them that everything they had and needed would come from Him. Remember how they gathered extra and God caused it to spoil? They were so afraid of not having enough that they failed to remember that God would give them what they needed when they needed it. The same applies to us.

Read 1 Chronicles 29:11 in the margin. Underline the phrase that indicates what belongs to God.

What are the possessions that you tend to think of as belonging to you rather than God?

my stuff
my children   *but it's*
my job   *all yours*
and I am
just your instrument

Recently, I had to clean out the attic of the home that I lived in for over twenty years. Downsizing from a five-bedroom home to a small two-bedroom apartment meant that I had to let go of many things because it wasn't possible to keep everything. While there were sentimental items from my daughters' growing up years and our family's past, I chose to let go and find my treasure in the memories rather than make the stuff my treasure.

"Did you know that the more you hold on to what you possess, the less peace you have?"[20]

—Andy Stanley,
How to Be Rich

Yours, LORD, is
the greatness and
the power
and the glory and
the majesty and
the splendor,
for everything in
heaven and earth
is yours.
Yours LORD, is the
kingdom;
you are exalted
as head over all.
(1 Chronicles 29:11)

When we see that everything is God's and merely ours to manage, then we think differently about what we buy and what we hold on to. Some of those emotional ties that we have may need to be taken captive, especially when our emotions won't let us let go of our stuff. Once our hearts stop being tied to our possessions, we are free from the pressure and panic of trying to get and keep things "just in case."

God helps us to keep the right perspective on our stuff by instructing us to regularly and willingly practice letting go of a small portion of what He has given us.

Read Malachi 3:10-11. What does God say about giving in these verses?

give it to God

What is His promise when we let go of our resources and give back to Him?

God will bless you beyond your imagination

Today's lesson challenges you to trust God with everything that you have and everything that you're dreaming about. It's not wrong to buy or own possessions; however, your goal is to never let your possessions possess you!

Extra Challenge

This week, give away something that you're uncomfortable letting go of, whether it's money, a special possession, or your time. Reflect on your experience below:

What did you do?

How did it feel to let go of something that was uncomfortable to give away?

What did you experience after giving generously?

Prayer

God, You are so generous to me! For all the times I fear not having enough money, time, or control, You are steadily taking care of me and providing my needs. God, I want to open my hands and my heart to be as generous as You are to me. Help me to honor You in this way. In Jesus' name. Amen.

Letting go of Expectations

Matthew 4:8-9 — *The devil tempts Jesus the 3rd time*

Luke 15:13-14, 17 — *The prodigal son*

Mark 8:36 — *"What good is it for someone to gain the whole world, yet forfeit the soul?"*

We will never find ___*happiness*___ in power, people, places, or things. But we will find peace and joy and purpose in ___*God*___.

Deuteronomy 6:13-14

Fear the Lord your God, serve only him + take you oaths in his name. Do not follow other gods, the gods of the peoples around you.

There is nothing wrong with having good things, but it is our hearts and our minds that must always move toward ___*worshipping God*___, so that God can do things in us and through us that have ___*eternal impact*___.

God promises us so much more!!

Tool #1 Q-tip – Quit taking it ___*personally*___. *What does this take?*

We have these expectations about the way people should behave.

Tool #2 Keep your eyes on your own ___*hula hoop*___

inside of my hula hoop are my responsibilities

cpu

Tool #3 What other people ___*think*___ of me isn't any of my business.

We are worried what other people think of us

it's not about us

"It's good for me to be aware of what people think, but I have to be careful about how much I care about what other people think."

What God thinks of me is most imp

Surrender Principle #4

Trusting God's promises will ___*bless*___ me, but pushing my plans will ___*stress*___ me.

A   I am way loved

B elieve that God is for you

C hallenge yourself to
          trust God +
          let go .

Denise

April 13th

Week 5

Living Like Jesus

(Matthew 4:11)

Memory Verse

"Not by might nor by power, but by my Spirit," says the Lord *Almighty.*
(Zechariah 4:6)

In the wilderness, Jesus surrendered all. His are the footsteps that we need to follow.

I'm always inspired when I read the stories of people who have surrendered all to Christ and whom God has used in such powerful ways.

One of my favorite songs was written by a man who struggled with surrendering all to God. Judson Van DeVenter was born in Dundee, Michigan, less than thirty minutes from where I live in Northwest Ohio. He became an art teacher and was active in his church. People around Judson recognized his talents and encouraged him to pursue full-time ministry, yet he was conflicted. "For some time, I had struggled between developing my talents in the field of art and going into full-time evangelistic work. At last the pivotal hour of my life came, and I surrendered all."[1]

Judson's song "I Surrender All" was published in 1896. Check out how many times the word *surrender* and *all* appear in just the first stanza and chorus:

> All to Jesus I surrender,
> all to Him I freely give;
> I will ever love and trust Him,
> in His presence daily live.
>
> I surrender all, I surrender all;
> all to thee my blessed Savior,
> I surrender all.

If you look up the lyrics to the entire song, you'll see that each stanza begins with, "All to Jesus I surrender," and the word *all* is included forty-three times. This song is all about surrender! Perhaps the secret to the hymn's enduring popularity is the number of times we must sing the words "I surrender all." Just singing it once isn't enough!

Judson's act of surrender, giving up his plans for his life to follow God's plan, not only changed Judson's life but also unleashed previously uncovered gifts and talents. Here's what he wrote: "A new day was ushered into my life. I became an evangelist and discovered down deep in my soul a talent hitherto unknown to me. God had hidden a song in my heart, and touching a tender chord, he caused me to sing."[2]

This week we're going to look at how to live a life of surrender like Jesus, as well as how Jesus knew when to accept help from others. When we're going through troubles and trials, it's vital to let others help us when we need it!

Day 1: Living like Jesus

Daily Surrender Prayer:

God, I choose to surrender

_____

_____

_____

to You today.

As I'm writing this, several tear-stained kitchen napkins lay crumpled next to my laptop. If you don't mind, I'm going to slip off my hat as your Bible teacher and write to you for a few moments as a fellow sister in Christ having a particularly hard day in a long wilderness season.

Today I'm fighting for surrender. No matter how much or how often I've practiced letting go, there are times when I'm tightly gripping the desire to have my own way. Letting go is a continuous act of faith, and it's not easy—even for a long-time Jesus girl like me. Over the past few years, I've let go of so many things so many times. Sometimes I get tired of letting go; so on a day like today, my heart rebels a little. But my heart also remembers that letting go is my only path to peace. It's when I let go that I can reach for God's hand to hold me and guide me toward His peace and blessing. Surrender is hard heart work.

Still, even in my weak moments, I remember that Jesus understands. When I reflect on what Jesus faced in the wilderness, I find comfort in knowing that I am not alone. Neither are you. So, if you've flopped over on the couch today and cried, "I can't do this," know this: Jesus understands. He really does.

Living like Jesus isn't about being perfect; it is about surrendering our lives and trusting that God knows exactly what He's doing every step of the way.

Let's review the three temptations and what Jesus models for us about surrender:

Temptation #1: *Satan tempted Jesus to use His divine powers to satisfy His human nature.*

Triumph: *Jesus surrendered His human desires to His divine nature.*

Temptation #2: *Satan tempted Jesus to force God to intervene outside of God's promises and rescue Jesus from reckless behavior.*

Triumph: *Jesus surrendered His circumstances and time line to God, even though he knew that the outcome would include pain and suffering.*

Temptation #3: *Satan tempted Jesus to give up His divine position for power and possessions.*

Triumph: *Jesus humbly surrendered His divine position to God's authority.*

We can be encouraged when we reflect on Jesus' triumphs over Satan's temptation. Most of all, we are reminded that when we live like Jesus and allow the power of God's Holy Spirit to flow in and through us, we can triumph, too! Victory in Jesus is possible, no matter what you are facing today.

After the wilderness experience, was Satan through tempting Jesus? In Luke's Gospel we find some insight into the answer, which has application for our lives as well.

Read Luke 4:13 in the margin. What does this verse tell you about what Jesus would face in the future?

When the devil had finished tempting Jesus, he left him until the next opportunity came.
(Luke 4:13 NLT)

In *The Message* translation, Luke 4:13 says, "The Devil retreated temporarily, lying in wait for another opportunity." This means that Satan showed up with other temptations that Jesus would have to face. The remedy for each future temptation rested in the same word that brought Jesus victory in the wilderness: *surrender*.

Though He never uses the word surrender, the principles of *surrender* are evident throughout Jesus' ministry, from His time in the wilderness all the way to the cross. In Mark 8 we see Jesus teaching and healing, and when they come to Caesarea Philippi, He asks the disciples who they say that He is. Peter declares Jesus to be the Messiah (Mark 8:29), and Jesus responds by saying that He must suffer and be killed in the near future. When Peter protests that their teacher would be killed by the religious leaders, Jesus rebukes him, saying, "Get behind me, Satan!" (Mark 8:33). This brings us to Mark 8:34, where Jesus begins to teach about what it means to live like Him.

Extra Insights

If anything, each victory we experience only makes Satan try harder.[3]

_____

"The word *Christ* means 'the Anointed One, the promised Messiah.'"[4]

Read Mark 8:34-37, and answer the following questions:

Who is Jesus speaking to?

Jesus says that a disciple must "_____ themselves and take up their _____ and _____ me"
(Mark 8:34).

Here Jesus defines what it means to be a disciple, and in many ways this portion of Scripture defines what it means to live the surrendered life. While we've become accustomed to seeing crosses hanging in churches and around our necks as fancy jewelry, crosses were violent tools of death in Jesus' day. In a modern context, imagine receiving a necklace with a little electric chair charm hanging on the chain. Disturbing!

Jesus doesn't want to sugarcoat what he's about to face and what those who follow him will face. As one scholar writes, "If there was a cross in *his* future, there would be one in *their* future as well."[5]

Let's unpack verse 34:

1. Deny themselves—Let go of their personal agenda.
2. Take up their cross—Let go of old beliefs, attitudes, and behaviors.
3. Follow me—Be obedient to God in all of His ways.

Consider Jesus' declaration of what it means to be His disciple and to live a life of surrender. What's the hardest part about this for you? Why?

When we're seeking to control, power is our drug of choice. Most of us won't admit that, because we're mostly nice people who want to love Jesus; but that doesn't change the fact that we don't want to give up our power. If change is a disease or an ailment that we don't like or can't manage, we'll shoot ourselves up with as many power boosts as we can in order to fight that change.

Living like Jesus means that you must be willing to give up your power to have your own way, even when you feel like you have good reasons to have your own way. Now, this isn't the same as giving up your power for someone to hurt you or put you in peril. Yet, just like Judson, your unconditional yes to God opens up the opportunity for incredible new gifts, opportunities, and adventures along the way.

There's a paradox around what it means to live the surrendered life that Jesus explains.

Write John 12:25 below:

Those who love their life will lose it & those who care nothing for their flesh will keep it in eternity

What application does this verse have for your life right now?

Give up "power". Encourage peace.

God saves us from ourselves when we let Him. God saves us from our selfish desires. He saves us from sinful attitudes, behaviors, and character defects that can destroy our lives and our relationships. Most of all, when our hands are open, God takes hold of us and leads us on a journey of maximum joy, peace, and fulfillment.

Just as in Judson Van DeVenter's life, there are gifts and talents within you that God is waiting to bring to the surface and use to have an impact in the world—and to bless you.

Memory Verse Reflection

> *"Not by might nor by power, but by my Spirit," says the* Lord *Almighty.*
> *(Zechariah 4:6)*

As you continue to reflect on what it means to live like Jesus and let go of circumstances that you can't control, this week's memory verse is a powerful reminder that there are things that only God can do.

This week's memory verse (Zechariah 4:6) is part of a vision that God gave to a young leader and prophet named Zechariah. Described as "the most Messianic of all Old Testament books," the Book of Zechariah contains eight references to the coming Christ in the New Testament.[6]

At that time, there was only a remnant, or small number, of God's people living in Judah after seventy years of captivity. They were trying to rebuild the temple and restore their way of life, but the process was long and hard. They had limited resources, and their leader, Zerubbabel, was discouraged because of the attitudes of the people around him and outside threats from others.

In the midst of all of these challenges, the angel speaks Zechariah 4:6 to the prophet: "'Not by might nor by power, but by my Spirit,' says the Lord Almighty." It is a reminder that while we can put in our best human effort and even accomplish some good things, there are certain things that only God can do or accomplish.

How does this week's memory verse apply to a situation that you're facing today?

Prayer

Complete the prayer below, indicating what you need to "lose" today so that you can live more like Jesus:

Dear God, thank You for Jesus' example in the wilderness and the victory that Jesus experienced when He surrendered His desires to You.

In response to Jesus' words in John 12:25, I want to deny my desire to fix or control wak circumstances *. In order to do this, I have to lose the following attitude or behavior:* not c in my cntrl pride, anger .

God, I trust that even though I don't know what You will do in the future, I am willing to trust that what You teach me in this wilderness season will bless my life and bring glory to Your name in the future. In Jesus' name. Amen.

Day 2: It's Okay to Accept Help!

Daily Surrender Prayer:

God, I choose to surrender

_____

_____

_____

to You today.

Is it hard for you to accept help? It can be for me.

In today's study we're going to see how Jesus accepted and embraced the help of ministering angels. Not only that, but we'll explore some of the reasons why control-loving people struggle to acknowledge their need for help or accept help when it is freely offered. At many times, I've been one of those people.

After years of counseling, prayer, and input from trusted, godly voices around the addiction issue threatening our family, I had to make the difficult decision to move out of my home. As family and friends continued to pray with me that a miracle would prevent that from happening, those same friends and family reached out to ask if they could help me with the move.

As much as I appreciated their love and support, I declined their offers of help. I didn't want them to see me completely broken down that day, so I used some control-loving tactics to politely but firmly deny their requests.

A few days before the move, a friend sent another gently worded text: "I just want you to know that I am here and I would like to help."

After that text, I felt the conviction of the Holy Spirit. I felt a whisper that sounded like, "Are you going to make this about you? When your daughters look back on that difficult day, they need to remember that they saw the hands and feet of Jesus loving and taking care of them."

As I was trying to control my move and protect myself from the embarrassment of falling apart, God needed me to surrender my self-centered behavior and consider His greater plan at work. He wanted me and my girls to be surrounded by His love shown through the hands of His people. In my efforts to control that day, I would rob my daughters of Jesus-loving friends and family who could love and serve them. They needed to see that God was taking care of them even though our prayers weren't answered as we'd hoped.

God sent many friends and family to fill my little apartment with His love on that very hard day. Whether it was someone storing meals in my freezer, putting together our beds, or lining the kitchen cabinets, God's love and mercy moved all around us. Even as I lay with my face on the floor in tears, I knew that God showed His love for me through the people who were there.

How hard is it for you to ask for help or accept help when it is offered?

___ Not hard at all   ✓ Somewhat hard   ___ Very hard

If you struggle with asking for help or accepting help, can you identify some of the reasons behind that struggle? Write them below:

Look up Matthew 4:11. Who came to attend to Jesus?

the angels

Angels came to attend to Jesus after His wilderness ordeal. To be honest, I didn't think about this verse much until I was hit with the realization that Jesus accepted the help of ministering angels. He said yes to the assistance and comfort they came to provide.

Jesus' willing acceptance of the angels' ministry leaves such an impression upon me. Even as Jesus is divine, He humbly recognized when His human strength—both physical and emotional—was depleted. He didn't push away the angels, saying, "I've got this," "Don't worry about me," "I'll be okay," or "I'm sure that there are other people out there who need more help than me."

The wilderness isn't the only time angels came to minister to Jesus. They also came when Jesus was in the garden of Gethsemane facing the excruciating stress of knowing what was to come—the realization not only that there would be pain and suffering but also that He would take on the sin of all humanity. While all four Gospel writers record the events in the garden of Gethsemane, only Luke records this important detail: "An angel from heaven appeared to Him and strengthened Him" (Luke 22:43).

Read Hebrews 1:14 in the margin. How are angels described? What is their role?

Are not all angels ministering spirits sent to serve those who will inherit salvation?
(Hebrews 1:14)

Angels are created spirit beings whose purpose is to worship and serve God (Psalm 103:21). In Hebrews 1:14, a key word to describe their activity and interactions with humanity is *ministering*, or serving, in various roles.

There's a lot of conversation about angels' activity in our world. Not only do we read about the activity of angels in the Bible but there also are a lot of stories that people tell about their encounters and experiences with angels. In the Bible, God uses angels to accomplish specific tasks.

Read the following verses, and assign the correct role to each Scripture, writing it in the blank.

Caring   Protecting
Delivering   Communicating a message

1. 1 Kings 19:5-7   _____

2. Psalm 91:11-12   _____

3. Hebrews 2:2   _____

4. Acts 5:19   _____

While angels are supernatural beings with "superhuman knowledge and power,"[7] they aren't superior to Jesus (see 2 Samuel 14:17, 20; 2 Peter 2:11; 2 Thessalonians 1:7). However, the supernatural ministering roles of angels are quite similar to the serving roles that we should offer to one other, especially to those who share our faith (Galatians 6:10).

Read the following verses, and summarize how each says we should minister to one another:

2 Corinthians 1:4 _____

Ephesians 4:29 _____

Hebrews 3:13 _____

What are your thoughts about accepting help or support when it is offered to you?

When you offer help to someone, do you sometimes silently judge or criticize them for not having the strength or being too tired to do it for themselves? How does this speak to your attitude about accepting help from others?

Is there an area of your life where you need to let your guard down in order to let others minister to you? If so, write about it briefly:

When I am going through a hard season or difficult trial, the ministry of my Christian brothers and sisters is what keeps me encouraged to keep going. The one who helps and the one who is helped both get to give glory to God! As I've thought about the angels ministering to Jesus, I've come to realize this: accepting help from others when I'm down or feeling weak can actually be an act of worship that allows me to give glory to God.

As I remember how much I am encouraged by those who minister to me, I'm motivated to minister to others. A few weeks after I moved into my apartment, a sweet friend lost her husband in a tragic accident. There were some complicated matters prior to his untimely death that most of her friends and family weren't aware of. A few days after his funeral, I sent her a message inviting her over for dinner at my apartment. She accepted the invitation, I think, because she knew what I was going through. That evening we sat and talked over dinner, and I felt the privilege of being a safe person she could talk to openly and honestly about what she was going through and the questions she had for God. To me, that dinner was exactly the kind of one-on-one ministry that makes the most difference in the world!

As much as we think we need to share our stories in a book, on a stage, or in some other large arena, I've discovered that God uses my story (my testimony) most powerfully when I sit one-on-one with someone or when I pray with someone. Here are some of my favorite ways to let God's glory shine through my wilderness story:

- sending a card
- calling or texting
- taking a friend out for coffee and listening
- sending a prayer via email
- sharing blog posts, Scripture verses, and even funny posts on my social media
- inviting a friend over for dinner, or taking dinner to her.

Can you think of someone right now who is going through a hard time and needs some encouragement? If so, which of the above can you do for her next week?

Trials or wilderness seasons feel isolating because it's really hard to explain what you're feeling or going through. But you aren't meant to go through the wilderness season alone!

The following exercise outlines a group of intentional friendships that I maintain in my life, especially during wilderness seasons. A circle of intentional friends can support your desire to live like Jesus during all seasons of life and help you get back on track when you struggle through hard times.

Exercise: Circle of Friends

Read each description and fill in the name of a friend who fits that description, or write a few names of women who might potentially fill that role in your life:

Mentor Friend
A Jesus-loving woman whose footsteps you want to follow in.
_____

Adventurous Friend
She encourages you to try new things or gets excited with you about new opportunities.
_____

Cautious Friend
She helps you think through challenging details or identifies potential yellow flags.
_____

"Ride or Die" Friend
She's a friend whom you can trust with your deepest secrets and struggles.
_____

Praying Friend
She doesn't give a lot of advice or input, but she'll be praying for you!
_____

A few things to note:

1. Be patient! It takes time to cultivate these intentional friendships.
2. These friends may not be connected to one another and that's okay because each woman is connected to you.
3. You don't have to talk to each woman in your circle daily, but definitely stay in touch with them.
4. Be interested in her life! Make sure to pray for her and ask God to give her wisdom to speak into your life.

If Jesus embraced the helping of ministering angels, then we can say yes when friends, family, or even strangers offer to help us in our time of need. Rather than worry about keeping score or trying to figure out how to pay someone back for their generosity, let others be a blessing to you. In return, you'll have plenty of opportunities to be a blessing to others.

Prayer

God, when I am weak, that's when Your power shines through my life the strongest for Your glory. Today, as I reflect on where I am barely hanging in there, I pray for the humility to say yes to help when it is offered. I choose to be like Jesus and let someone serve me during a weary time. In Jesus' name. Amen.

Day 3: Praying like Jesus

Do you remember the movie *War Room* that came out a few years ago? I remember going to see the movie with a friend. I loved seeing Priscilla Shirer's character evolve from struggling to pray to embracing a life of prayer. That night I went home, cleared out my office closet, and turned it into my own little prayer war room. I pushed in a little stool to sit on. The next morning, I began taping notecards of Bible verses, prayer requests, and unanswered prayers to the walls of that closet.

After years of struggling to reverse my tendency to do-first-pray-second, that little prayer room was just the setup that I needed. Too often I prayed in the places where my control-loving fingers itched to make things better. But in that little prayer closet, it was just me and God. I could settle in and give Him direct access to my heart because my hands were no longer busy.

Take a look in the margin on the next page for a simple yet profound explanation regarding the purpose of prayer that has been used to help even those who don't want to believe in God begin to talk to Him.

Daily Surrender Prayer:

God, I choose to surrender

———————

———————

———————

to You today.

I don't know how hard or how easy prayer comes to you. If you love to pray, that's awesome! You've been blessed with a special gift, and I hope that you use it well. For those who are like me with prayer requiring more effort, it's a pursuit that's absolutely worth it!

Living like Jesus means praying and talking to God on a regular basis. Today, we're going to consider what that looks like, especially when it comes to the prayer of surrender.

The Gospel writers capture Jesus' prayer habits and locations for us.

In the following verses, identify where Jesus prayed and anything unique about that prayer time. I completed the first one for you.

	Where did Jesus pray?	Anything unique?
Matthew 14:23	Mountain	He was alone
Mark 1:35		
Luke 5:16		
Luke 6:12		

If there was ever anyone who had a nonstop agenda, it was Jesus! He could have spent all of his time on earth doing all the things. Yet over and over again, Jesus demonstrates the value of praying for and doing later. Counseling a man who wanted to turn toward God after killing his son-in-law while drunk, Martin Luther gave the man some simple yet profound guidelines for prayer: "It is a good thing to let prayer be the first business of the morning and the last at night. Guard yourselves against those false, deluding ideas which tell you, 'Wait a little while. I will pray in an hour; first I must attend to this or that.'"[9]

This is so important for me to remember because it's so easy to believe that I have to accomplish my to-do list. However, the reality is that when I pray, God focuses my heart and mind so that I can do better things instead of trying to make things better.

Throughout Jesus' time on earth, we see Him praying in various locations and circumstances. What would Jesus need to pray about? Let's consider three reasons Jesus prayed, and they are the same reasons we need to pray like Jesus.

1. Connection to God

Here's a challenging question: why did Jesus need to pray? After all, Jesus was fully divine, possessing all the qualities of God (Philippians 2:6; Hebrews 1:3). Yet, Jesus was fully human as well (Luke 1:31; Philippians 2:7). The Bible makes reference to Jesus' development as a human being, learning wisdom and obedience (Luke 2:52; Hebrews 5:8). The intersection between Jesus' divinity and his humanity is the topic of all kinds of scholarly writings; however, practically speaking, Jesus prayed because He wanted to stay connected to God. The outcome of that connection empowered Jesus' human nature to endure the difficulties of human life.

One of the most well-known prayers in the world is The Lord's Prayer. This is a prayer about how we can connect with God as "our Father." Notice the section about how Jesus prays about temptation.

> [9] *"This, then, is how you should pray:*
> *"'Our Father in heaven,*
> *hallowed be your name,*
> [10] *your kingdom come,*
> *your will be done,*
> *on earth as it is in heaven.*
> [11] *Give us today our daily bread.*
> [12] *And forgive us our debts,*
> *as we also have forgiven our debtors.*
> [13] *And lead us not into temptation,*
> *but deliver us from the evil one.'"*
> (Matthew 6:9-13)

List what Jesus teaches us to pray for and about:

How connected to God do you feel when you pray? What are some of the difficulties or distractions, either around you or in your mind, that keep you from feeling connected to God?

Did you notice that you can pray for God to spare you from temptation? "Jesus' model prayer...shows us that we can ask the Father to spare us from temptations, to help us resist those things that would trip us up, and to rescue and save us from the enemy."[10]

Extra Insight

"We see clearly in the gospels that Jesus' life of prayer showed up in his life of power."
–Jennifer Kennedy Dean[11]

2. Preparation and Gratitude

Do you believe that God can lead you and guide your steps? I do! The challenge for me is to slow down and create space for that to happen. Can God guide us while we're on the run? Absolutely! But, I've found that as I prioritize praying about an upcoming speaking event, a relationship issue, or a major decision, I'm leaving vital space for the Holy Spirit to impress upon my heart or mind wisdom, solutions, spiritual insights or even fresh ideas. The more space I leave for God to speak into my life, the more that I hear from Him!

Perhaps this gives us insight into why Jesus prayed before key moments in ministry as well as before making decisions.

Look up the following verses and make note of some key moments:

Matthew 15:36 _____

Luke 6:12-13 _____

Luke 10:21 _____

What is the benefit of taking time to pray before tackling a problem?

Give thanks to the LORD, for he is good; his love endures forever.
(1 Chronicles 16:34)

Read Philippians 4:6-7 below, and circle the phrase "in every situation."

Give thanks in all circumstances; for this is God's will for you in Christ Jesus.
(1 Thessalonians 5:18)

⁶Do not be anxious about anything, but in every situation, by prayer and petition, with thanksgiving, present your requests to God. ⁷And the peace of God, which transcends all understanding, will guard your hearts and your minds in Christ Jesus.

Jesus lived in a state of gratitude, meaning that He was thankful at all times, not just when life was going His way.

And whatever you do, whether in word or deed, do it all in the name of the Lord Jesus, giving thanks to God the Father through him.
(Colossians 3:17)

Read the verses in the margin. How does giving thanks help you keep perspective while you're dealing with a problem?

3. Live Out Purpose

For me, it's Jesus' prayer in the garden of Gethsemane that is the best example of prayer to live out our purpose. There are times when living for God is hard, especially when we know that following God's way is going to cost us or lead to hardship or heartache.

Jesus came to earth to seek and save the lost. Yet, as a human being, He struggled with what surrender would cost Him; so He prayed to God for help and strength to live out his purpose.

Read Matthew 26:36-38. Where did Jesus and the disciples go to pray?

Summarize what Jesus told three of His disciples about how He was feeling.

The name of the garden, Gethsemane, comes from an Aramaic word meaning "oil press."[12] Olives were collected, crushed, and the oil gathered at this site. The meaning of the garden is symbolic because Jesus came to pray in this place where olives were crushed. Now, Jesus faces His own personal crushing, prophesied by the prophet Isaiah long ago: "But he was pierced for our transgressions, he was crushed for our iniquities; the punishment that brought us peace was on him, and by his wounds we are healed" (Isaiah 53:5).

Jesus lets the disciples know the extent of the stress He was feeling. He truly understands the great pressures we face in life! Another follower, a physician named Luke, also records Jesus' human response to the extreme stress and agony of knowing what lies ahead: "His sweat was like drops of blood falling to the ground" (Luke 22:44).

Read Matthew 26:39-44.

What is the prayer that Jesus prays in verse 39?

How many times did Jesus pray that same prayer in these verses?

Extra Insight

"There is a rare physical phenomenon known as *hematidrosis*, in which, under great emotional stress, the tiny blood vessels rupture in the sweat glands and produce a mixture of blood and sweat."[13]

What words or phrases did Jesus use in His prayer to affirm that he was willing do what God sent Him to do?

Just as Jesus went willingly with the Holy Spirit to be tempted in the wilderness and willingly allowed Satan to tempt Him from the top of the temple, Jesus went willingly into the garden of Gethsemane knowing that the time had come for Him to fulfill his earthly purpose. But it doesn't mean that this was easy for Jesus.

This is one of my favorite stories in the Bible because Jesus' human reaction to extreme stress shows us that He understands how much strong emotions can overwhelm us. I also love this story because Jesus prays the same prayer of surrender not once, not twice, but three times. Sometimes it's so hard to surrender!

Is there someone or something or some situation in your life that you've tried to surrender but keep holding on to because you're afraid to wholly and completely surrender? If so, write about it briefly:

Jesus' prayers hold the key to what we need to know about letting go even in the hardest situations. As He speaks "not my will, but your will be done" in the garden, He not only surrenders the future pages of His life story to God but also positions Himself to fully experience the glory of God—even though it won't seem that way at first.

Read Hebrews 5:7-8, and summarize these verses in a few sentences:

Jesus didn't pray because He wanted God to do His will. Jesus prayed so that He stayed in step with God's will. Jesus knew that the cost of surrender would be His life.

Surrender feels scary if we're only looking at what we might lose. It feels suffocating when we feel like letting go is sentencing our dream to death. For years I tried to force solutions because I couldn't see past my deep pain in order to see our family's situation through God's perspective. The first step of my journey to let go of control-loving behaviors was to fully and wholly embrace Surrender Principle #1: I am not in control of others or outcomes. Then I could take my eyes off my own plans and finally begin trusting in God's promises not only for me but also for my family.

Keeping Prayer Simple

Prayer is a powerful act of surrender, especially for those of us who want to be in control! Author Anne Lamott expresses this so well when she said, "Most good honest prayers remind me that I am not in charge, that I cannot fix anything, and that I open myself to be helped by something, some force, some friends, something *something*...I am clueless, but something isn't."[14] This kind of honest prayer doesn't need to be complicated or lengthy. In fact, keeping it simple often can help us to be more open and authentic in our conversations with God.

There are several popular frameworks that can help you to keep prayer simple and yet personal and real. Here's one of the most well-known models:

A – Adoration (Tell God how much you appreciate Him.)
C – Confession (Tell God about your mistakes, failures, and struggles.)
T – Thanks (Acknowledge the blessings that God has given to you or others.)
S – Supplication (Ask God for what you or others need.)

Take a few moments and use the ACTS acronym to pray, making notes below. Or, if you prefer, write a prayer of surrender for anything in your life that you might be struggling to let go of:

Sometimes we can be reluctant to pray when fear strikes, wanting instead to swing into action with control-loving behaviors. But that is when we most need to stop and pray. This brings us to our next surrender principle.

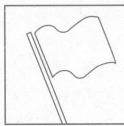

SURRENDER PRINCIPLE #5

When fear tempts me to flee, fix, or force my way,
I will choose to stop and pray.

This surrender principle is inspired by Philippians 4:6-7, which you looked at earlier in the lesson. This verse provides a practical and powerful template to help you pray instead of panic.

It's not a sin to feel fear, especially when you're facing something overwhelming or scary. Rather than run away or resort to control-loving ways, you always have the opportunity to pray. You can use the ACTS technique or another simple prayer tool I call the CALM Technique, which I share in my book *Winning the Worry Battle*:[15]

> **C**ount to five by inhaling on the number and exhaling the word *Mississippi*.
>
> **A**cknowledge God's presence by saying, "God, I know that you are here with me."
>
> **L**ist where you need God's help.
>
> **M**editate and repeat the following: "God is here, and He will take care of me/this."

After I wrote about the CALM prayer technique in *Winning the Worry Battle*, I added a final thought that is worth repeating here, especially if you're feeling insecure: *I am safe when I believe God knows what is best for me and those I love*. God knows what He is doing and even when life doesn't make sense, God will guide you and give you peace and power along the way.

Prayer

Dear God, as I think about how to let go and live like Jesus, help me to apply the lessons I've learned from Jesus' life about where I need to hold on, let go, or even just wait for You to deal with the things I cannot control. In Jesus' name. Amen.

Day 4: Forgive like Jesus

God, I choose to surrender

_____

_____

_____

to You today.

In two major wilderness seasons of my life, letting go of the hurts and pain that people caused has been a major part of my journey. I've also had to let go of punishing myself for the times when I failed, controlled, or hurt others too.

Whenever I've given messages on forgiveness, whether at a conference or as a guest speaker at a church, people will stop me in the hallway or send me messages afterward that say: "Barb, I want to forgive, but I can't. I just don't know how to let go of what they did."

I've had times in life when I've felt the same way. How could I forgive those who have caused me tremendous pain or took away something in my life that I could never get back? There are times when I haven't wanted to forgive because I felt justified in letting my anger burn. My anger was a way of trying to control those who hurt me. My fear was that if I gave up my anger, then I could be hurt again. (Both of which are untrue.)

Jesus faced betrayal by Judas, one of the people closest to Him. Jesus endured criticism and even attempts on His life from the religious leaders. Jesus was rejected over and over by people who didn't believe that He was the Messiah.

And yet, for all of the pain that humanity caused Him, Jesus still died on the cross so that everything we've ever done wrong and ever will do could be forgiven.

Today we're going to look at what it means for us to forgive like Jesus. While you may not be ready to let go of and forgive those who've hurt you, I pray that today's study of God's Word helps you take a step in that direction.

We're going to begin with a powerful lesson that Jesus teaches all of us who tend to think that others need forgiveness more than we do.

Read Luke 7:37-38. How was the woman described?

What did the woman do when she showed up at the home where Jesus was eating?

Some translations call her an immoral woman. She's a woman who knows that she has made mistakes, and she isn't trying to hide them. Perhaps you know what it feels like to be this woman. You have shameful secrets,, or your shameful secrets have been found out. As you read about the woman wiping Jesus' feet with her tears, you understand because you've cried many tears over your mistakes as well. Yet there is something beautiful about someone who is real about who she is rather than hiding her mistakes. I admire this woman because she brought her truest self to Jesus.

Read Luke 7:39-43.

How was Simon testing Jesus? Why was he so critical of Jesus? (v. 39)

What was the point of the story that Jesus told him? (vv. 41-43)

As a religious leader, Simon was no doubt thinking of the laws that this sinful woman may have broken because of her lifestyle and choices. He may or may not have known her full background, but he judged her just the same.

Why do you think we find it so easy to judge others' motives and behaviors?

Jesus points out to Simon that the person who has the most need of forgiveness has the most gratitude for being forgiven. Then Jesus indicates that the sinful woman is actually more loving than the religious man who prided himself on following all of the rules, because she has been forgiven so much.

What is Jesus' main point to Simon in Luke 7:47?

Essentially Jesus is saying that our ability to forgive and love others is tied to just how much we recognize that we've been forgiven. When we truly realize how much we have sinned against God, we realize how much we need to be forgiven ourselves; and that gives us perspective.

If we're focused only on the wrong that people have done toward us, we can easily fall into the snare of the comparison trap. (Please know that I'm not discounting any of the trauma you've suffered, only that Scripture says we all have sinned and fallen short of God's perfect standard [Romans 3:23].)

Read Romans 5:12 in the margin. What do we learn about how sin entered the world?

Therefore, just as sin entered the world through one man, and death through sin, and in this way death came to all people, because all sinned.
(Romans 5:12)

Read Colossians 1:13 in the margin. How did God rescue us from the sin that separates us from Him?

For he has rescued us from the dominion of darkness and brought us into the kingdom of the Son he loves.
(Colossians 1:13)

Since God has rescued and restored you through Jesus Christ, what difference has that made in your life?

If that last question was hard to answer, you aren't alone. We don't often reflect on what God has rescued us from—especially if we have grown up in the church. Those who come to saving faith in high school, college, or adulthood tend to have inspiring examples of what God rescued them from. I love hearing those stories because those individuals give God so much glory, recognizing just how much they've been forgiven!

In some of my other Bible studies, I've written about my grandmother, Magnolia, and her struggle to forgive my grandfather after his long-term affair that ended their marriage. After the divorce, Grandma held on to the pain and anger, and eventually the bitterness inside her created several serious health conditions, including bleeding ulcers. It took my grandmother a long time to finally let go of her anger. Thankfully, she lived the rest of her life overflowing with joy and love for others.

Forgiveness is a key part of what it means to follow God in all of His ways.

Read 1 John 4:20-21. Why can't we say that we love God and hate others?

Write Colossians 3:13-14 below. Is there anyone in your life right now that you need to let go and forgive? If so and you are struggling with forgiveness, what's holding you back?

There was a time in life when I was angry over a situation where I felt like some people had wronged our family. One of the people involved apologized, but I really didn't know the others involved. We experienced some negative consequences from the offense, and every time I felt the pain of what had happened to us, I burned with anger inside. There were times when I would daydream that something bad would happen to them so that they might feel the same kind of pain that I did.

At the time, I'd just started working for my church. While I wasn't in a teaching or leadership role back then, I still figured that it probably wasn't a good idea for me to be so full of anger all the time. However, it was so hard for me to forgive because our family kept feeling the pain and consequences of what happened to us.

I picked up Stormie Omartian's classic book *The Power of a Praying Woman*, in which she writes about Jesus' response to Peter's question about how often he is to forgive someone:

> Jesus answered, "I tell you, not seven times, but seventy-seven times."
> (Matthew 18:22)

Here Jesus removed the limits on forgiveness that Jewish tradition taught. Stormie proposed that if an incident kept coming to mind and made forgiveness hard, then perhaps it would be helpful to express forgiveness each time the incident came to mind.

I took her advice. Every time I began to feel anger toward the people involved, I began to say, "I forgive you." I didn't say this to the people involved; I didn't send a text or email. I simply whispered those three words to the thought or memory.

This took discipline. At first, I said those three words many times reluctantly before I ever believed them. After a week, I was more consistent in being willing to say them even though I still felt the pain. It took about six weeks before

I realized that I wasn't having as many angry and bitter thoughts throughout the day.

The blessing in letting go of my resentment and anger was that, down the road, I developed precious relationships with people I might have missed out on if I had not let go of my anger.

I've used this approach at other times in my life when I've been hurt or when memories of hurt and pain have persisted. Jesus knew that just saying "I forgive you" once wouldn't be enough for the kind of pain that we experience in relationship with one another.

Is there a place in your life where this approach might be helpful? If so, will you commit to try it just for today?

____ I'm willing to try it   ____ I'm not ready to try it yet

Read Romans 12:17-21. How are we instructed to let go of payback behaviors?

Fill in the blanks:

"Do not _____ anyone evil for evil." (v. 17)

"As far as it depends on you, live at _____ with

_____." (v. 18)

"Do not take _____." (v. 19)

"If your _____ is hungry, feed him." (v. 20)

"Do not be overcome by _____, but overcome

evil with good." (v. 21)

My encouragement to you today is to let the truths of what Jesus taught sink into your heart and mind. When it comes to forgiveness, I've learned that if I wait until I feel like forgiving, I may never get around to it. Forgive in obedience and leave the rest up to God. I'm not going to say that you will *feel* better about what happened to you; however, you will experience the blessing that comes with being obedient to what God has called you to do.

Prayer

Dear God, You know what hurts and You know who hurt me. I know that I need to forgive and let go, but I can't do it without Your help. God, help me to see just how much You've forgiven me, and help me to let go and forgive others. In Jesus' name. Amen.

An Important Note

If a crime has been committed against you and the authorities should be involved, don't let anyone shame or guilt you out of reporting a crime.

**Daily
Surrender
Prayer:**

*God, I choose
to surrender*

_____

_____

_____

to You today.

Day 5: Hope like Jesus

If you're anywhere near a church or a group of Jesus-loving people and you hear someone say, "God is good," chances are you'll hear the reply, "All the time!"

For some, hearing that familiar chant sounds like a cliché because life can be hard, and sometimes we don't feel like God is good when our life is hard. But what if both can be true at the same time? Is it possible that God is good *and* life is hard?

There is the way that we think life should be, and then there is the way that life is. For many of us, the quest is to fix or force life into the way we think it should be—except we can't.

One of the lessons we learn in living like Jesus is how to live with the tension of accepting that life is never going to be exactly how we want it to be and yet living each day full of hope and joy! Jesus knew how to live with the tension of what I like to call "holding hope and heartache in both hands." He saw the depravity of our sinful world along with our pain and suffering, yet He also proclaimed hope and peace for all who want to step out in faith and trust Him.

If you've been defining your life by either good or bad, today's study is an invitation to become like Jesus and learn how to hold on to both hope and heartache at the same time.

Read John 14:27 in the margin. What is the message that Jesus gives to His disciples about what they would encounter in life and the perspective that they must hold on to?

"Peace I leave with you; my peace I give you. I do not give to you as the world gives. Do not let your hearts be troubled and do not be afraid."
(John 14:27)

Within that verse, Jesus teaches that His gift of peace transcends the problems and pain we experience in life. When we have peace, or inner calm, about the unknown future, then we are assured that we will be okay, no matter the outcome, even if the outcome is difficult or disappointing. Too often we think that our problems have to be solved before we experience peace, but Jesus teaches us that peace is a gift we're to access and enjoy even in the midst of great difficulty.

One of the best examples of this came from one of the women in the pilot group for this study. A few months before the group began, she discovered that her husband of over twenty years was having an affair. He moved out of the house and, at this time, he has no plans to return to their family. As we talked about how to think more like Jesus, she made the following statement about where God has led her during the surrender journey: "I don't understand the way that I am right now. Even though I have no clue about what's going to happen, I have God's peace. It's amazing. Rather than be shattered, Jesus is making me stronger than I've ever been."

Read Philippians 4:7 in the margin. How is the peace that God provides described here?

And the peace of God, which transcends all understanding, will guard your hearts and your minds in Christ Jesus.
(Philippians 4:7)

Can you think of a time when you've experienced God's peace even though your circumstances were out of control or didn't make sense? If so, describe it briefly:

Franciscan friar Richard Rohr explains the mindset where two opposing situations can be true at the same time as "non-dualistic thinking," or the ability to think beyond an "all or nothing" mentality.[16] In contrast, examples of dualistic thinking are when we use superlatives such as "best," "worst," "greatest," or "only." Non-dualistic thinking recognizes that something bad can happen and something good can happen in the same situation at the same time, and we can mourn and celebrate both. As Rohr says, "This is all true and we can still be happy."[17]

Can you think of an example of holding both hope and heartache in your life?

How does accepting good and bad at the same time help us to accept the gift of peace that Jesus offers?

What is at risk if we believe that we can only experience peace when life is good?

During my surrender journey, I've had to let go of defining my life by extremes. When I define my life by good or bad, it's like a pendulum swinging back and forth all day long—my thoughts, emotions, and actions swinging to extremes. It's exhausting!

Instead, I want to look at life like a railroad track, as Rick Warren suggests. He explains that there will never be a time when life will only be good or life will only be bad. Instead, Warren says that life is like railroad tracks in that there's good and bad always happening at the same time.[18]

Here's a railroad track that symbolizes your life. Label one track "best" and the other track "worst." Then on the wooden ties between the tracks, write events or circumstances that include both good and bad.

For many years I hosted a women's Bible study on Thursdays in my office at the church where I worked. I loved this Bible study because it was diverse in race, age, and life circumstances. Each week I'd begin the study by asking the ladies to share their "celebrations and struggles." We'd go around the room and share one area of our lives that was going well or that we wanted to brag about, and then we'd share another area of our lives that was hard or heartbreaking. It was important to me that the women in my group could talk about the good and bad in their lives. Sharing both the good and bad invited each woman to show up as her truest, most authentic self; and each week we were reminded that no one's life is perfect and no one's life is all bad.

Why is it important for us to share both the good and bad in our lives?

The classic hymn "It Is Well with My Soul" has endured for over a century, and new generations now experience the original words set to new arrangements of updated music. However, the backstory of the song remains the same.

After enjoying financial and career success as a Chicago lawyer in the 1800s, Horatio Spafford lost his real estate fortune in the Great Chicago Fire of 1871. A Christian, Spafford made plans for his family to join the great evangelist Dwight Moody in Great Britain. In November 1873, Spafford's wife and four daughters set sail to Europe, but Spafford had to stay behind at the last minute. As the tragedy unfolds, the ship carrying Spafford's family was hit by another ship and sank in only twelve minutes. All four of his daughters died, joining in death a son who had passed away only a few years before. His wife survived and sent her husband a message that simply read, "Saved alone."[19]

It is believed that Spafford wrote the words to the hymn while his ship crossed over the area where the other ship supposedly sank. The hymn begins,

> When peace like a river attendeth my way,
> when sorrows like sea billows roll;
> whatever my lot, thou hast taught me to say,
> It is well, it is well with my soul.

Spafford's song is a beautiful example of holding hope and heartache with both hands. He'd suffered a devastating tragedy, yet Spafford held on to a hope that held his soul in a place of peace. The result is that he could proclaim that it was well with his soul.

Read Romans 8:18-25. Notice wherever you see the word *hope*.
According to this verse, what are the things that we can have hope for in the future?

Because of sin, our world suffers. But when we were saved, we were given hope (v. 24). You've got a lot to look forward to if you are a child of God! Here's what we have to look forward to:

- being released from sin and suffering;
- receiving full rights as children of God; and
- being given new bodies!

As much as we have hope for the future, that doesn't mean that our hardest and most difficult problems on this earth will go away. I've known a number of people in my lifetime who've suffered for decades with a chronic medical condition, a difficult marriage for nearly fifty years, or a defiant child who became a self-destructive adult. Can we have hope even when our trial never seems to end?

In 2 Corinthians 12, Paul writes of experiencing a tremendous, unidentifiable pain that he refers to as his "thorn in my flesh." There has been lots of speculation around what the specifics of Paul's problem could have been. All we know is that the issue that tormented Paul is described as a "messenger from Satan" (2 Corinthians 12:7), which means that it was pretty bad.

Read 2 Corinthians 12:8-10, and answer the following questions:

How many times did Paul pray for God to take away his "thorn in the flesh"? (v. 8)

Write God's response to Paul in verse 9:

What did Paul discover about his weaknesses? (v. 10)

How would you explain what Paul means when he says, "For when I am weak, then I am strong" (v. 10)?

For the past few years, one of the comments that I've heard most often is, "Barb, you are so strong." This comment never ceases to amaze me. The truth is that I am not strong, but I can see where God's strength shines through me! It is the power of God that shines through my tears, my trials, and the incredible triumphs of my life. Because I am weak, I've become strong in God. Amen!

In what ways have you seen your weaknesses make you strong in God's power?

Embracing hope and heartache at the same time has reshaped my perspective in so many ways. While my heart has shattered countless times over what's happened to my family, at the same time, I've learned how to rejoice in God's goodness and to enjoy the blessings that surround me every day.

God has led me to this perspective and I pray that He leads you toward it as well. As we live in that precious perspective we can sing, "It is well with our soul!" and give God glory no matter the circumstances of our story.

Prayer

Dear God, thank You for the hope that You give us for the future! Help me to live in the tension that not everything is going to be all good and to remember that not everything is all bad. Instead, I want to remember the hope that You are with me and for me. Most of all, I claim the promises that one day You will make everything as it should be. I'm praising You for that today. In Jesus' name. Amen.

Week 5 Video Viewer Guide

Isaiah 53:3 *He was despised + rejected by man*

Psalm 34:18 *The Lord is close to the brokenhearted + saves those that are crushed in spirit*

John 16:33 *In this world you will have trouble but I have overcome*

Genesis 50:20 *what was meant to hurt us God will use for glory*

Romans 8:38-39

① ___Praying___ ing like Jesus. — *drew to lonely places to pray*
   ② *He had a lifetime of prayer ~>*
   ___Forgiving___ like Jesus. *Posting*

Grace is there for all of us

Luke 7:41-43 — *story of those who lent $*
   —> the one c greater debt forgiven is the one most grateful

Ephesians 4:32 *Be kind + compassionate to one another forgiving just as Christ forgives you.*

Living like Jesus means holding ___hope___ and ___heartache___ in both hands.

Surrender Principle #5

When fear tempts me to flee, fix, or force my way, I will choose to ___stop___ and ___pray___.

We are always
loved

We will trust
that God will
take care of us

Remember scorekeeping
⤷
Barbara Johnson

Week 6

Blessings of the Surrendered Life

(Isaiah 61:3; Ephesians 3:20; 1 Peter 5:7)

Memory Verse

He fills my life with good things.
(Psalm 103:5 NLT)

I met Kim Fredrickson in October 2014 in Monterrey, California, at my literary agency retreat. Kim and her husband, David, sat next to me at dinner that first night. Immediately, I heard a familiar pumping sound coming from the oxygen tank by Kim's side. I shared with Kim that the pumping noise reminded me of my Aunt Mary's oxygen pump and my gratitude for the technology that has extended her life with us. During a later conversation, Kim told me how self-conscious she was over the machine and the noise. She was grateful that I acknowledged the pump that night and made her feel more comfortable.

In 2013, Kim fought an aggressive form of breast cancer. Less than a week after finishing nine months of cancer treatment, Kim developed shortness of breath. In 2014, she was diagnosed with pulmonary fibrosis, a rare lung disease with a five-year life expectancy without a transplant. Unfortunately, Kim had to be cancer-free for five years before she'd even be considered as a transplant candidate.

While Kim's life-threatening illness seemed dramatic, she was at complete peace with the circumstances of her life, even as difficult as they were. She had to retire from her career as a marriage and family therapist, but she decided to keep writing to help others. She told me,

> I know God has a purpose for this in my life, and in the lives of others. I honestly wish I didn't have to go through cancer or pulmonary fibrosis. I wish I would have a miraculous healing. If that doesn't happen, I can accept this because I know God doesn't waste any pain or hardships as I submit to Him and allow Him to use what has happened in my life for maturity in my own life and as an example to others.

> Life isn't supposed to be easy, and I don't feel ripped off by God. He has blessed me in so many ways, even in the midst of such a devastating time. I know He has lots of plans of how this will impact others in ways that I will never know about until heaven. I don't need to know what those plans are. I trust Him.

Kim inspired me because she wasn't embarrassed by her powerlessness; rather, she glowed with God's power. She couldn't travel to do speaking events, but she hosted online weekly Facebook Live sessions to encourage, equip, and educate others from her home when she was feeling well enough to do so.

In 2018, Kim announced that she'd made it to the all-important, five-year cancer-free milestone. After months of testing, Kim made it on the transplant list and began waiting for a set of lungs. However, by the spring of 2019, Kim's lungs could no longer function on their own. She spent three months in the hospital waiting for a set of donor lungs, but that was not to be. Kim passed away in June 2019.

I'm inspired by Kim's decision to live the surrendered life even though she was powerless over her medical condition and didn't get the happy ending she was hoping for. Kim experienced the blessing of seeing God use her life to do more than she could ever ask or imagine on her own.

This is the blessing of the surrendered life.

Day 1: The Blessing of *Kintsukuroi*

Extra Insight

"Gold was one of the first metals known to humankind....It never tarnishes—a property that makes it ideal for jewelry....Gold is mentioned over 500 times in the Bible, more than any other metal."[3]

Although living the surrendered life asks us to open our hands to receive the beautiful blessings that God wants to give us, we still grapple with what to do with pieces of our lives that are changed, transformed, or perhaps missing from who we were before. Here's a helpful visual that I think best describes the brokenness and the beauty of the surrendered life.

In the fifteenth century, the ruler of Japan, Ashikaga Yoshimasa, broke a favored teacup. It must have meant a lot to Yoshimasa because he sent it to Chinese craftsmen and insisted they repair it. Imagine the pressure of a powerful military leader demanding that his favorite teacup be repaired!

Rather than use unattractive yet conventional repair techniques for their time, the artists employed some creativity and assembled the cracked pieces by bonding them together with powdered gold mixed into a bonding agent. Repairing the broken pieces of pottery with gold turned into a new art form called *kintsugi* (kint-su-gee), which has come to symbolize the philosophy that "broken objects are not something to hide but to display with pride."[1]

The repaired work of art is called *kintsukuroi* (kint-su-ku-roy), which means "more beautiful for being broken."[2] In our conventional thinking, we want to hide the cracks. However, when you look at photos of pieces of *kintsukuroi*, the cracks are actually showcased. Before the tragic moment, the ceramic piece of pottery was used for normal tasks; but once the gold was applied, the value of the piece exceeded the cost of the original piece.

Praise God that He is the master craftsman! He sees not only our broken pieces, but God knows just how to fit those jagged edges back together. God grabs those pieces and He makes us whole again! God knows how to reassemble the little bits and pieces that we have given up on. Most of all, when God puts us back together, He doesn't just walk away and hope that we keep it together. What's so beautiful is that God holds us together with Himself. God holds us together with His peace, His provision, and His protection so that, even in a difficult world, people can see His glory shining through the broken places in our lives.

When God holds us together with Himself, people notice that, although life should have beaten us down, we are standing strong and courageous. Rather than defining ourselves by our brokenness, we surrender the broken pieces of our lives to God and let Him do His work.

Read 1 Peter 1:7 in the margin. Why does God allow His people to go through tests that feel like fire? What is it about gold that is so desirable or attractive?

*Trials allow us to see how genuine our faith is - to purify us
Gold is valuable/precious like our faith*

Now read Isaiah 61:3 in the margin. Hard times don't last forever! What does God exchange our hardship and heartache for when we trust Him?

Joy, a crown of glory a garment of praise

will make us strong

Read Ephesians 3:16-20, and complete the following:

1. **God uses His glorious riches to** *empower* **us. (v. 16)** *c̄ inner strength through the spirit*

2. **What does the writer want us to grasp about God's love? (v. 17-18)**

God's love is total. It reaches every place in our ♥.

3. **What surpasses knowledge? (v. 19)**

The love of Christ

4. **See verse 20 below. Underline the phrase "immeasurably more," and circle the word *all*.**

Now to him who is able to do <u>immeasurably more</u> than (all) we ask or imagine, according to his power that is at work within us.

(Ephesians 3:20)

These trials will show that your faith is genuine. It is being tested as **fire** tests and purifies **gold**—though your faith is far more precious than mere **gold**. So when your faith remains strong through many trials, it will bring you much praise and glory and honor on the day when Jesus Christ is revealed to the whole world.

(1 Peter 1:7 NLT, emphasis added)

[The Lord has sent me to]…provide for those who grieve in Zion— to bestow on them a crown of beauty
    instead of ashes,
the oil of joy
    instead of mourning,
and a garment
of praise
    instead of a spirit
    of despair.

(Isaiah 61:3)

As you've moved through your wilderness season and have grown in your courage, strength, perseverance, or faith, you've realized the increase in the power of God at work in you. This means that you can have the expectation that God will do even more in your life because God's power is working more in your life.

As God continues to work in your life, what are some of your God-sized dreams?

Are there any special passions, gifts, or abilities that have come to the forefront as a result of what you've been through or are going through? If so, write about them briefly:

Can you think of a next step for you to begin allowing God to use you and what you've been through? (If you're not ready for that step, that's okay too.)

Too often we overfocus on the broken pieces of our lives, and sometimes we see our identity as a reflection of those broken pieces—labeling ourselves things such as the "woman who can't lose weight," "divorcée," "childless woman," "the woman who changed her major multiple times and dropped out of school," and so forth. As author Jennifer Renee Watson says in her book *Freedom: The Gutsy Pursuit of Breakthrough and Life Beyond It*: "Brokenness is not the ending; it's the beginning of something beautiful inside of you being rebuilt. It looks like gratitude rather than guilt."[4]

If you've been walking with God through trials and wilderness seasons, God's power is radiating through you even in the midst of your circumstances. Rather than just seeing yourself as broken or out of service due to circumstances, perhaps it's time to create a new picture of your whole self. Like the art form kintsugi, God can restore and redeem the most difficult parts of your life.

EXERCISE: Creating Your Spiritual *Kintsukuroi*

1. Look at the bowl below. Within each cracked section, list a broken area of your life. For example, you could write in your childhood, financial hardship, loss of health, a relationship failure, a moral failing, a parenting disappointment, and so on.

2. Along the cracks themselves, write a lesson, an aha moment about God, or a key Scripture verse that has strengthened your faith or given you courage. If you need some help, consider phrases such as "gained courage," "developed persistence," "found my faith," "experienced God's supernatural intervention," "began fasting," or "started praying more." *(For example, in one of the broken areas I would write "broken family," and along one of the cracks I would write "experienced God's loving presence.")*

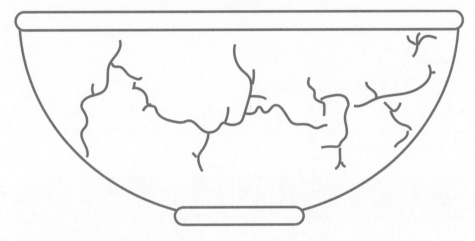

Memory Verse Reflection

> *He fills my life with good things.*
> (Psalm 103:5 NLT)

This week's memory verse was written by King David. One commentator notes that this song of praise may have been written in David's later years as he had grown to see the magnitude of God's glory in his life.[5]

If you know anything about David's life, you know he slayed a giant as a young man before spending fifteen or so years of his life on the run in the wilderness from King Saul before finally becoming king of Israel. Even after becoming king, David's life had many ups and downs, including drama with adult children and his disastrous affair with Bathsheba. I don't know what kind of drama your life has had lately, but David seems like the kind of guy who would understand.

It's especially sweet that David would write the words found in Psalm 103:5, saying that God fills his life with good things. In other words, David discovered the true gift of satisfaction with God. David's life didn't have to be perfect for him to realize the abundance of God's blessing, even in the broken places of his life.

How would you describe the "good things" that God has filled your life with?

I'm so grateful that God can take the broken pieces of our lives and bring beauty from them. No matter if you're in a wilderness season, experiencing a difficult trial, or trying to heal from the past, give God the broken pieces and trust that He won't leave you broken. Rather, He'll lovingly and gently heal and hold you together with Himself. If you need a daily reminder of this, I'd encourage you to make or buy kitsugi for yourself.

Prayer

Dear God, I am so grateful that You put all of the broken pieces of my life together to make me whole in You. I'm so grateful that I don't have to fix myself! All I need to do today is pick up the broken pieces of my life and surrender them to You. I am so grateful for that! In Jesus' name. Amen.

Day 2: The Blessing of Supernatural Provision

Daily Surrender Prayer:

God, I choose to surrender

_____

_____

to You today.

Throughout the study we've looked at several stories of the Israelites' forty years of wandering the wilderness. There were multiple supernatural stories of how God took care of the former slaves who had to learn how to be faithful to God over four decades in the desert. One of my favorite parts of the Israelites' time in the wilderness is that their clothes never wore out that entire time (Deuteronomy 8:4; 29:5). I sure wish that my favorite jeans could last that long!

As the Israelites prepared to enter the Promised Land, Moses recapped their time in the wilderness and reminded them of the following:

> *For the LORD your God has blessed you in everything you have done. He has watched your every step through this great wilderness. During these forty years, the LORD your God has been with you, and you have lacked nothing."*
>
> (Deuteronomy 2:7 NLT)

I wonder if the average Israelite man or woman listening to Moses' address really felt that way? After all, there were many instances when God expressed anger and disappointment over their lack of faithfulness, evidenced by their complaints that they were going to starve or die of thirst. Yet Moses reflects an important truth for all of us: *God will be faithful to us, even when we aren't faithful to Him.* I don't know about you, but I praise God for that!

[handwritten: God is always faithful]

God is always at work taking care of us but, unfortunately, we often miss it. Is it even possible for us to see all that God does to take care of us? John Piper tweeted, "God is always doing 10,000 things in your life, and you may be aware of three of them."[6]

One of the blessings we discover in the Christian life is that once we pull back on our control-loving tendencies, we get to see God's work in our lives more clearly. When we're not busy trying to fix others or outcomes, we're able to experience the jaw-dropping awe of watching God care for and carry us through the situations that were out of our control to begin with. That's one of the beautiful blessings of the surrendered life!

Let's look at a time when Jesus supernaturally provided for a group of people. The elements of this story have a parallel relationship to the saga of the Israelites in the wilderness.

Read Mark 6:34-37. In verse 34, what is the word used to describe how Jesus felt toward the people?

[handwritten: Compassion]

Why did the disciples get upset when Jesus told them to feed the people?

[handwritten: Not enough food or $]

At the end of a long day, Jesus knew that the people would be tired and hungry. I love that Jesus not only showed compassion toward their spiritual needs but also their physical needs too! However, the disciples protested because to feed a crowd that size would require more money than they had available.

Oh, how many times have we looked at a situation and declared it impossible because we didn't have the money that we needed? Jesus was standing right next to them and they still stressed out about not having enough.

You may already know the story, but I invite you to read what happens next with fresh eyes—and then we will tie this story to the Israelites' experience for some unique insights.

Read Mark 6:38-44, and fill in the blanks.

The disciples told Jesus that there were _____ *five* _____ loaves and
_____ *2* _____ fish available. (v. 38)

Jesus lifted up the loaves and fish to heaven and gave
_____ *blessed/gave* _____ *thanks* (v. 41)

The people ate and were _____ *filled* _____ . (v. 42)

The disciples picked up _____ *12* _____ baskets of broken
pieces of bread and fish. (v. 43)

There were _____ *5,000* _____ men who ate that day. (v. 44)
+ their families

This is one of the most popular stories in the Bible. Yet when I consider what the disciples must have felt as they looked around at thousands of people while Jesus lifted up five loaves and two fish, I'm thinking that they might have been raising their eyebrows at one another wondering what was going to happen when they ran out of food after the first two people ate.

This story parallels the Israelites in the wilderness in a few ways. Here is a summary of one scholar's observations:

1. Like Jesus' disciples, Moses felt pressured to feed the complaining Israelites right before God sent all of those quail (Numbers 11:22).

2. There were only two small fish, which draws a similarity to the manna God provided. Neither seemed like much, but combined with God's supernatural provision, it was enough.

3. There is a difference here in that God instructed the people not to collect the leftover manna, but Jesus instructs that the leftover bread and fish be collected so that people could see that there was more than enough.[7]

As you reflect on how Jesus took so little and God used it to supernaturally provide for thousands, what does this speak to you about whatever you're worried about today? (Consider not only financial needs but needs for God's supernatural provision across every area of your life.)

Read Matthew 6:8 and Matthew 6:32 in the margin. What does God already know?

He Knows what we need

This means that, right in this moment, God is completely clear on what you need. This also means that tomorrow, God will know exactly what you need. Our challenge is to remember that God often takes care of our needs in unexpected ways.

In 1 Kings 17:7-12, God sends the prophet Elijah to the home of a widow for food. Once Elijah requests some water and bread, the widow informs him that she's about to make one final meal for herself and her son because they will die of starvation after that. However, Elijah gives the woman a prophecy of supernatural provision.

Read 1 Kings 17:13-16, and answer the following questions:

Who does Elijah instruct the widow to feed first?

to make Elijah bread

What is the prophecy that Elijah gives the widow? (v. 14)

that the jar of oil + container of flour will not run out

What happened to the jar of flour and jug of oil? (v. 16)

Never was empty

Right before Elijah came to the widow's house, he was hiding out by a brook, and God had sent ravens to feed him. The brook dried up, and God sent Elijah on to a new place of provision.

In her Bible study *Elijah: Spiritual Stamina in Every Season*, Melissa Spoelstra observes that the widow actually fed Elijah before feeding her son. That's a big deal! I love what Melissa says about God's supernatural provision in our lives: "But as I have found to be true in the life of my own family, God often uses unlikely sources to provide for us. These unlikely sources remind us not to trust in logic or riches. God is always our source."[8]

One of my favorite supernatural stories of provision in my own life happened about twenty years ago. As I lay in bed one night, I prayed to God about some of the things that I wanted to do for my child but wasn't able to because of high private school tuition and tight finances. However, I told God about what I wished that I could do for the upcoming Memorial Day holiday weekend. Then I thanked Him for what He'd already done for us before going to sleep.

Do not be like them, for your Father knows what you need before you ask him.
(Matthew 6:8)

For the pagans run after all these things, and your heavenly Father knows that you need them.
(Matthew 6:32)

The next morning, I went into work and stopped by my mailbox. I hadn't said anything to anyone about my prayer the night before. In fact, I didn't want anyone to know about the budget crunch. In my mailbox was a white envelope with my name printed on the front. When I opened it up, there was a single hundred-dollar bill inside.

To this day, I have no idea who left that gift, but it was a reminder that God provides supernaturally—and even surprisingly.

Can you recall a time of God's supernatural provision in your life, whether it was financial or an opportunity that you couldn't make happen on your own? If so, write about it briefly:

Made sure Paul was diagnosed + taken care of

I was young and now I am old,
  yet I have never
  seen the righteous
  forsaken
  or their children
  begging bread.
        (Psalm 37:25)

my Context

Read Psalm 37:25 and James 1:17 in the margin. What do these verses tell us about God provision?

Imagine for a moment that you have complete trust that God is going to provide what you need in whatever situation you may be worrying about or trying to fix. What would that feel like?

Calm
Peaceful
   but may not be my
      outcome . Surrender

Every good and perfect gift is from above, coming down from the Father of the heavenly lights, who does not change like shifting shadows.
        (James 1:17)

Read the following verses, and write God's promises to provide for His people:

Psalm 34:10

God will provide for our needs

Matthew 7:7

Keep asking .

Philippians 4:19

God will meet all of my needs through Jesus.

Another supernatural provision happened in my life a few years ago. Every few months, my friend and fellow Bible study author Melissa Spoelstra and I meet at a coffee shop located halfway between our hometowns in Ohio. One day, as we talked about our families and ministries, I mentioned that I'd applied to speak at a nationally known speaking and writing conference, but it was a long shot for me to get in. Always the encourager, Melissa said that she'd pray over that opportunity for me.

A week later, Melissa called with an incredible story. She was speaking at an event in Arizona when the coordinator of the conference I applied to showed up at her event. She lived in Arizona and stopped by Melissa's event to meet with another speaker. Melissa ended up riding in the car with her for two hours. As the two women got to know each other, Melissa realized the connection and mentioned our conversation the week before.

A few days later, I received an email from the conference coordinator who said that she could see God's divine hand working in this situation. She offered me an opportunity to be a workshop presenter the following year.

God put all of the people and pieces into place. I didn't have to push or pressure anything.

Is there something today that you really hope God will supply? If so, write a prayer below, and use one of the verses from today's study as part of the prayer.

Help me ⁓ the right words God. I am not sure of how to say this

Today's a great day to give yourself the gift of celebrating God's supernatural provision in your life. Give thanks to God because, as my grandma used to say, "God can make a way out of no way" and that's the truth! I hope that today's lesson also gives you hope if you're waiting in circumstances where you don't know where the money, help, or connections will come from. While you may not know how He will provide, keep praying and trusting that He can!

Prayer

Dear God, You can do all things, including doing so supernaturally, to provide for what I need, but can't provide for myself. As Psalm 121 says, my help comes from the Lord, the Maker of heaven and earth. I'm reminded today that if You can create the world, You can take care of ___the difficult conversations___ in my life today. I will trust in You. Amen.

Day 3: The Blessing of Divine Protection

Daily Surrender Prayer:

God, I choose to surrender

_____

_____

_____

to You today.

Recently I traveled to El Paso, Texas, to welcome home my daughter Kate from her most recent military deployment. I had prayed all year long for her safety, and I was so grateful to see her and spend time with her. On the last morning of my visit, we were at a bookstore when a gunman walked into a nearby Walmart and opened fire, killing twenty-two people and injuring many more. We made it out of the area safely but were shaken by such a tragedy. I returned home that day, only to wake up the next morning to news of another shooting overnight in Dayton, Ohio, which is two hours from where I live.

As I posted about the El Paso event on social media, many kind friends expressed their thankfulness that we were okay. Some expressed comments such as praising God that He had protected us. While I appreciated and understood the care and concern behind those comments, I felt an uncomfortable tension. I wondered, *Should we define God's protection by how safe He keeps us?*

If you grew up in church like me, you heard or perhaps even prayed, "God, please put a hedge of protection around them," or "God, I'm praying that you keep them safe." There's nothing wrong with those prayer requests, but here's a question for us: Is the blessing of God's protection limited to keeping us and our loved ones safe, or is the blessing that we experience God's power in all circumstances?

God's protection isn't about keeping us safe. There are stories of brave martyrs from ancient times through our present day who died doing what God called them to do. Therefore, it seems that God's protection is His eternal presence while we do what He's called us to do. God's protection can be found in His timing and through His guiding hand—even when our plans fall apart or we're rejected or we encounter physical danger. However, if we define God's protection as staying safe, we may circle the wagons and live in fear, missing out on serving others.

Have you ever turned down an opportunity to serve others because you were afraid of the risk?

What are some of the things that you fear not having control over if you say yes to helping others or serving in a new ministry?

If you are holding back from serving, God may be calling you to let go of trying to keep your life safe. He has a "divine assignment" that only you can do, and you're missing out on the blessing that God has waiting just for you.

What if you dropped your "be safe" mentality and stepped outside of your comfort zone? Perhaps your daily surrender this week is to open your hands to that divine assignment and let go of your fears, surrender any control-loving issues, and leave the outcome to God.

If you had no fear, where would you want to serve God and others?

In the past I've written about my reluctance to go on an overseas mission trip. My church sends six to eight teams a year to countries in Central America, Europe, and even a few countries that we can't talk about openly. In the years when I actively said no to participation, there was just one reason why. And it wasn't even a big reason. I rejected God's nudge to serve His people overseas because of my fear of spiders. It's embarrassing to talk about even now.

Yet a decade ago I realized that I had to say yes to God and surrender my fears of getting bitten, not knowing the language, being uneasy about staying in host homes, and being harmed. I remember that moment of surrender too. It was during a weekend message when I was teaching, and there was a point as I told the audience about my upcoming trip that I lifted my eyes to the ceiling of the auditorium and expressed my surrender to God. For a moment, all of the people seemed to fade away as I gave my fears to God.

That was a decade ago. I've been on ten overseas mission trips since then, and I'm still afraid of spiders. I've accepted that one day I might get bitten. I

Extra Insight

"How many times have I thought it was safety that mattered, when Jesus already died to save us? No one ever got saved unless someone else was willing to be unsafe."
—Ann Voskamp[9]

hope not, but I also know that I won't let a spider bite stop me from what God has called me to do.

After Jesus' time in the wilderness, there were many instances in His ministry when He was divinely protected from being captured or hurt by the religious leaders who wanted to silence His message. Yet God's supernatural power made it possible for Jesus to continue in the work that He came to do.

Read the following verses. How did Jesus get away each time?

Luke 4:30

He walked right through a croud

John 8:59

Jesus hd himself getting ready to be stoned

John 10:39

He escapes their grasp?

As one writer puts it, "Jesus remained elusive until His time finally arrived."[10] I love that Jesus didn't worry about His safety. This meant that the backroom schemes the religious leaders cooked up to trap Him didn't matter. Even in the garden of Gethsemane when Jesus felt those intense human emotions, He surrendered to God's ultimate plan rather than demand God prevent pain or death. There's a lesson about divine protection that seems to surface, and it's this: God promises that He is present no matter what you are going through. He'll be present with you through earthly difficulties, and even when life on earth ends for you, God promises that you'll be in His eternal presence in heaven. In Romans 8:38, we're reminded that nothing can ever separate believers from God's love for us, which includes His presence in our lives.

When the Israelites left Egypt, they'd never been in the wilderness before. They had been slaves their entire lives, so they likely had minimal knowledge of the area outside Egypt. And there were over one million Israelites—that's a lot of people to watch out for and care about in the dusty unknown wilderness. Yet God had a plan to protect His people even though they had no idea where they were going.

Read Exodus 13:20-22. In a previous lesson, you focused on how God took care of the Israelites. Again, how did God lead the Israelites during the day and at night?

If God had not guided the people, they would have been like thousands of factions of stray cats wandering in the desert. The Sinai Peninsula was a big place at over 23,000 square miles.[11] For people who'd never lived on their own or supported themselves, they needed God's protection. While we don't know the size of the cloud and fire pillars, they were big enough so that all God's people would see them when needed.

God's guidance is the best protection that we have in the wilderness season.

Read Psalm 119:105 in the margin. How is God's Word described?

a Lamp for my feet
a guide in my path

Your word is a lamp for my feet, a light on my path. (Psalm 119:105)

Think about the lamps in your home. How much light do they cast? Most lamps aren't created to fully light a room, just a specific section of the room. God knows that we can't handle His full revelation, and so for our protection He guides us with what we need to know when we need to know it.

A wilderness lesson that is reinforced for me over and over again is that often God's protection is just as much what He *doesn't* tell me as what He does tell me.

One of the most famous stories of the Israelites' protection in the wilderness is found in Exodus 17.

Read Exodus 17:8-13, and answer the following questions:

Who attacked the Israelites? (v. 8)

Amalaek

Who went with Moses up the hill while Joshua fought the enemy? (v. 10)

Aaron + Hur

What did Moses have to do so that the Israelites would keep winning? (v. 11)

hold up his staff

How did Aaron and Hur help Moses when he got tired? (v. 12)

What happened in verse 13?

Even as God took care of the Israelites in the desert by providing manna and making sure their clothes didn't wear out, the Israelites were still attacked by a formidable army. The same goes for us; God will take care of us during our wilderness journey, but sometimes we'll face an attack and need to fight.

Moses' arms seemed to indicate the success or failure of the Israelites as he prayed to God on their behalf while Joshua and the army fought on the battlefield. Moses interceded in prayer for the army and the strain of fervent prayer seemed to take tremendous energy because he needed Aaron and Hur's help to hold his arms up.

What if that battle would have ended differently? Could Moses still claim God's protection if the Israelites had lost that battle? Yes, if Moses defined God's protection as remembering God's constant presence in all circumstances, whether good or bad.

Like Moses, our goal is to lift our hands and pray to God, concentrating on His presence and power in our lives.

Many years ago, I won a sales award that included an all-expense trip to Africa for a week-long safari. As I spoke with one of my customers about the trip, I mentioned a few fears around the twenty-hour-long plane ride. I was trying not to think about the plane crashing, but I also couldn't *not* think about it. My customer mentioned that he would read and pray Psalm 91 whenever he took the long flight to Africa where he did missions work.

Psalm 91 is one of the most revered psalms of all the songs recorded in the Book of Psalms. Commentators suppose that Moses wrote this psalm that deals with all of the dangers that we face in life.

Read all of Psalm 91 in your Bible, and refer to the verses below to complete the chart:

[14]*"Because he loves me," says the* LORD, *"I will rescue him;*
    I will protect him, for he acknowledges my name.
[15]*He will call on me, and I will answer him;*
    I will be with him in trouble,
    I will deliver him and honor him.
[16]*With long life I will satisfy him*
    and show him my salvation."

(Psalm 91:14-16)

What will God do for us?	
v. 14	He will rescue us.
v. 14	He will protect me

[handwritten margin note: Remembering God's presence in all circumstances]

v. 15	Call on me
v. 15	He will be c̄ me in trouble
v. 15	He will deliver me + honor me
v. 16	He will satisfy me
v. 16	He will show me his salvation

Extra Insight

"Among [God's] blessings will be deliverance and protection, answered prayer…, companionship in times of trouble, honor, satisfaction and a long life."[12]

In what areas have you played it safe in the Christian life because you didn't want to be inconvenienced or face potential danger?

Have you ever stepped into a "divine assignment" and sensed God clearing the way for you to do what He called you to do? If so, write about it briefly:

Is there an opportunity or "divine assignment" that you may need to say yes to today? If so, write it below and identify the first step you can take to dive into that assignment.

Prayer

Dear God, thank You for Your divine protection that watches over us as we say yes to what You've called us to do. Help us to know that You are with us in all circumstances, and that we can trust in Your promises and goodness, even when we are afraid and full of doubt. In Jesus' name. Amen.

Day 4: The Blessing of Peace

How do we live surrendered like Jesus when there's still life to be lived and situations to be handled? Matthew 5 records Jesus' Sermon on the Mount, in which He teaches us how to live with godly attitude and character. In early translations, this section would be titled "The Beatitudes," or as some have called them, the "be-attitudes."

The Message translation of this section of Scripture rings with so many reminders of what it looks like to live the surrendered life and the blessings of peace with God that we experience along the way.

Read Matthew 5:3-11 below from *The Message* translation and answer the questions that follow:

³**"You're blessed when you're at the end of your rope. With less of you there is more of God and his rule.**

⁴**"You're blessed when you feel you've lost what is most dear to you. Only then can you be embraced by the One most dear to you.**

⁵**"You're blessed when you're content with just who you are—no more, no less. That's the moment you find yourselves proud owners of everything that can't be bought.**

⁶**"You're blessed when you've worked up a good appetite for God. He's food and drink in the best meal you'll ever eat.**

⁷**"You're blessed when you care. At the moment of being 'care-full,' you find yourselves cared for.**

⁸**"You're blessed when you get your inside world—your mind and heart—put right. Then you can see God in the outside world.**

⁹**"You're blessed when you can show people how to cooperate instead of compete or fight. That's when you discover who you really are, and your place in God's family.**

¹⁰**"You're blessed when your commitment to God provokes persecution. The persecution drives you even deeper into God's kingdom.**

¹¹"Not only that—count yourselves blessed every time people put you down or throw you out or speak lies about you to discredit me. What it means is that the truth is too close for comfort and they are uncomfortable."

(Matthew 5:3-11)

1. In each verse where it appears, underline the phrase "you're blessed" and draw an arrow from that phrase to the word *when*.

2. For each statement, circle the "letting go" action and draw a heart by the blessing that is received afterward.

3. Which "letting go" lesson stands out to you the most? Why?

4. Do any of the above verses (Matthew 5:3-11) "match" or correspond to the temptations that Jesus faced in the wilderness (Matthew 4)? If so, which ones?

Each of these "letting go" lessons Jesus teaches has transformed my life in powerful and unique ways. Here's what I've discovered: There are some lessons in life that I've learned and forgotten. However, whatever I learn in the long, hard wilderness season has never been forgotten. There's a "sticky" conviction that comes after great challenge. I'm sure that as Jesus taught the crowd on the hillside, they could hear that conviction in his voice. We know when someone has been through something. It's not just the words that they say but how they say them!

As Jesus continued to teach from the mountainside, He shared the bottom line as to *why* we need to let go and learn to live like Him in a world where so many are struggling.

Extra Insight

Salt brings out the flavor of food. It's an influencer that brings out the best in whatever it is poured on.

Read Matthew 5:13-16. What food enhancer does Jesus call His followers?

Salt

In verse 16, Jesus describes His disciples with another symbol. What is it?

Light

In this passage, considering both symbols—salt and light—how does Jesus want His disciples to influence the world with their godly attitudes and character?

As you consider the trials and testing that you've been through, how can you or your story uplift, influence, or encourage others even as you are going through a difficult time?

This brings us to our final surrender principle that points to the resolution that you have to make. You're always going to have problems, but if you want to experience peace and calm, you must choose God's process instead of your plan.

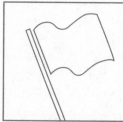

SURRENDER PRINCIPLE #6

Surrender is my only path to
God's peace, power, and provision.

We like to figure things. Yet it's often our determination and persistence to protect, fix, or force that creates hardship and heartache in our lives.

On the final week of our pilot group for this study, one of the ladies said that she had a pattern of letting go of certain situations for short periods of time and then jumping back into control-loving behaviors. Then things would get out of control and she would be devastated, so she would decide to let go again. On our last night, she threw up her hands and said, "That's it! I'm just gonna need to totally surrender and not try to take it back anymore. My heart can't keep going through this."

If you can relate, the good news is that total surrender is where we find God's peace, power, and provision. That is the blessing waiting for us!

Prayer

O God, I pray we would all have the aha moment when we realize that You are the only way that we can get what we've been working so hard for. Open our eyes to our need to surrender others and outcomes once and for all. In Jesus' name. Amen.

Day 5: The Surrendered Life

It's the last day of our study time together and I'm so glad that you've joined me for this experience. As we've learned how to give over what we can't control as well as what we've learned from the Israelites about what *not* to do, my hope and prayer is that you've learned what it means to let go and live like Jesus.

If you've really battled to let go, you aren't alone! As I talked with the women in the group who piloted this study, many of them talked about how much energy it takes to live surrendered. A few remarked about how easy it was to slip back into old behaviors if surrender wasn't a daily and intentional practice in their lives.

Perhaps you feel the same. Chances are there were days or weeks during this study experience where you really focused on opening your hands and letting go of fear, people-pleasing, entitlement, or regret. Maybe you experienced times when you felt like you were right back at the beginning of your journey and feeling guilty about not surrendering because you aren't ready to let go quite yet.

Whatever you feel and wherever you are at, can I encourage you to give yourself compassion if your surrender journey has some less-than-successful days? Like the Israelites' journey in the wilderness, sometimes we've got to go back to the same place more than once in order to learn what God wants to teach us. Repeating a lesson isn't a sign of failure; it's a beautiful second chance to grasp a blessing that God truly wants to give us.

Read Philippians 1:6. How long will God keep working on us?

Daily Surrender Prayer:

God, I choose to surrender

_____

_____

_____

to You today.

The beautiful news is that God will never give up on you! Whether you barely completed the pages of this study or you filled in every blank, God wants you to experience the freedom of surrender and He'll keep guiding you toward that goal. God was at work drawing you into this study experience and He'll continue His work long after this study is over.

Today I want to help you capture as many lessons as possible that you've learned through this study and your own wilderness season, whether you're still in it or you're on the other side. Even if you're on the other side and it has been awhile, it's good to see just how far God has brought you and to remember any blessings that you may have forgotten.

 Take a moment and flip back through this workbook. Note below any significant verses, stories, or questions you might have underlined. Record one or two aha moments or key encouragements that you experienced during the study.

It's a good thing to look back on difficult stretches in life; but we want to make sure that when we look back, we're reflecting on the right things. God knows that, as human beings, we have "negativity bias." That means, as one podcaster explained, "When it comes to remembering the bad stuff, our brains are like Velcro, but when it comes to remembering the good stuff, our brains are like Telflon."[14] It's our human nature to remember the bad and forget the good.

At the end of the Israelites' journey, Moses gathered the people one final time to help them remember God's goodness toward them and how they could continue to experience God's goodness in their new land.

The Israelites gathered as a community outside of the entrance of the Promised Land in Kadesh-Barnea. It's here that Moses gives his final message to the people, a long message captured in the Book of Deuteronomy. God's people had been through many years of hardship and heartache. Now that they were about to put all of that behind them and begin new lives in a new place as free people, God didn't want them to forget where they'd come from and what they'd been through. But most of all, He wanted them to remember how He'd gotten them through it all.

Truth be told, I never paid much attention to Deuteronomy until a few years ago. There are books of the Bible that seem like the popular people you like to follow on social media, such as Psalms, Proverbs, John, Romans, and a few others. But books such as Deuteronomy, Habakkuk, Philemon—well, these books are like your shy distant cousins with weird names. You figure they are probably pretty nice people but you just haven't taken the time to get to know them. But, if you do, you discover that they have a fascinating life of their own. Deuteronomy is one of those fascinating books, quoted over eighty times in the Old Testament![15]

Jesus valued the Book of Deuteronomy. In fact, all three of Jesus' responses to Satan in the wilderness (see Matthew 4:1-11) came from this book. Let's look at all three references from Deuteronomy that Jesus used to shut down Satan's temptation:

Look up each verse and write the key message:

Deuteronomy 8:3

Deuteronomy 6:16

Deuteronomy 6:13

One commentary observes that "Jesus and the apostles considered Deuteronomy of paramount importance to their own teaching about God and

His dealings with His chosen people and humanity at large."[16] It seems that the message of Deuteronomy contains lessons about a life of faith that transcends the generations from ancient times through Jesus' time on earth to our present life now. The message that the people heard from Moses is the same message that you and I need today.

Picture yourself as a woman who has been living in the desert for forty years. You might be tired of sand getting in all of your stuff, so stopping again for someone to give you a lot of instructions might make you impatient. No doubt there were those who were impatient among the Israelites. Yet I'd like to think that the crowd was mostly captivated because it would be the last time that they would hear from Moses. As the old generation began dying off in the wilderness after the rebellion (Numbers 13–14), the new generation would come to see Moses as the only leader whom they'd ever known.

What about Moses? Picture him standing before over a million people at the end of a forty-year odyssey. Can you imagine him speaking with great passion in front of the people? This was his farewell message to a group of people he had led and interceded for more than a few times. I imagine that his voice might have boomed with conviction, perhaps cracked slightly with emotion, but surely most of his words were clear, calling God's people to continue to be totally dependent on Him. That was *the* main lesson they should have learned in the wilderness.

As you reflect on the lessons that they should have learned, you also will reflect on some of the lessons that you've learned.

Read Deuteronomy 8:3-11 below, and underline the phrases that remind you of Jesus' responses to Satan in the wilderness:

³*He humbled you, causing you to hunger and then feeding you with manna, which neither you nor your ancestors had known, to teach you that man does not live on bread alone but on every word that comes from the mouth of the Lord. ⁴Your clothes did not wear out and your feet did not swell during these forty years. ⁵Know then in your heart that as a man disciplines his son, so the Lord your God disciplines you. ⁶Observe the commands of the Lord your God, walking in obedience to him and revering him. ⁷For the Lord your God is bringing you into a good land—a land with brooks, streams, and deep springs gushing out into the valleys and hills; ⁸a land with wheat and barley, vines and fig trees, pomegranates, olive oil and honey; ⁹a land where bread will not be scarce and you will lack nothing; a land where the rocks are iron and you can dig copper out of the hills.*

¹⁰*When you have eaten and are satisfied, praise the* L*ORD* *your God for the good land he has given you.* ¹¹*Be careful that you do not forget the* L*ORD* *your God, failing to observe his commands, his laws and his decrees that I am giving you this day.*

(Deuteronomy 8:3-11)

In verse 3, circle the phrase "He humbled you." When and how has God humbled you, when you realized that you didn't have the kind of control/power that you thought you had?

Reflect on verse 3 again. Think of a time of hardship or trial. When have you experienced God's supernatural provision?

Moses says that God teaches His children like a father disciplines his son (v. 5). What are some discipline/teaching moments that you remember from your own wilderness seasons?

Verse 6 discusses obedience, and Moses frames the reason for obedience so that the Israelites can enjoy the blessings that God has waiting for them (vv. 7-9). Times of trial force us to choose how we want to live and who we want to follow—usually a process that requires trial, error, and failure before correction.

Can you think of some areas of your life where you're walking in more obedience to God now than you were before this study? If so, what are they?

Why do you think Moses needs to remind the people not to forget God once life is good again? Can you think of some areas of your

spiritual life that cool off when you aren't feeling the heat of adversity?

As excited as we might be to leave a time of difficulty behind, I sometimes feel some reluctance to leave a wilderness season. Sounds crazy, but it's true. It's because I know that the wilderness is the place where I'm closest to God. In the wilderness, my life has been stripped down, and I think about whether or not I'll get so busy with rebuilding my life after the wilderness that I will let go of some of the lessons I've learned, filling my hands with other things.

In Matthew 22:37, Jesus drills down to the takeaway lesson that I've spent many years focusing on. This lesson is simple to remember and provides a framework that I can live out once I leave the wilderness and begin living toward God's next assignment for my life.

Read Matthew 22:37 in the margin, and circle the word *all* each time it appears.

In Matthew 22:37, Jesus references Deuteronomy 6:4 as the basis for His command. When I think about all of the lessons that I've learned in the wilderness, each of those lessons can be traced back to loving God more in each area of my life—whether it's learning how to let go of desiring things more than God (heart), learning how to worship God rather than pride (soul), or challenging my control-loving mentality in order to obediently submit to God's principles (mind).

I'm not sure how I've made it through my wilderness journey. It seems like the days faded into months and now, many years have passed. While I remember lots of hard days, what I remember more is God's goodness, faithfulness, protection, and love. These are the life-giving, life-transforming lessons that I consider a privilege to carry forward toward where God is leading me in the future. I hope that you feel the same.

As we close our time together, I would like to pray over you. Afterward, I encourage you to write out a final prayer declaring your decision to live the surrendered life.

God, thank You for walking with my friend through this experience. Whatever changes she has seen in her life, I praise You for them! I pray that in the days ahead, she will continue to let go and live like Jesus in everything that she says and does.

When she's tempted to keep score, I pray that You remind her to give grace.

When she's tempted to helicopter or micromanage, I pray that You remind her to trust.

"You must love the LORD your God with all your heart, all your soul, and all your mind."

(Matthew 22:37 NLT)

Extra Insight

Deuteronomy 6:4-9 is known as the *Shema*, which is a Jewish confession of faith. "These verses make up one of the most ancient features of worship among the Jewish people."[17]

When she's tempted to interrupt others or not respect their boundaries, I pray that You remind her to be humble.

When she's tempted to nag or offer unsolicited advice, I pray that You remind her to be wise and loving with her words.

When she's tempted to excessively plan, I pray that You reminder her to trust in Your provision and not to worry about her future.

Most of all God, I pray that she grabs onto and never lets go of Your enduring, faithful promises for her life and those that she loves.

Amen.

Prayer

In the space below and on the following page, write a prayer declaring your desire to live surrendered to God each day of your life. If there is a situation where you've struggled to let go of trying to control the outcome, ask God for the desire to let go. Finally, ask God about any opportunities where you might bring glory to Him through the story of what you've been through.

India ☐
Denise ☐
Michelle ☐
Ayisha ☐

My Prayer

Week 6 Video Viewer Guide

Surrender Principle #6

Surrender is my only path to God's _power_, _peace_, and _provision_.

What does it look like to live the surrendered life?

A trusting _heart_.

A peaceful _mind_.

Open _hands_.

The surrendered life is not about _perfection_. _priceless pieces of artwork_

It is God who _holds_ us _together_.

It's God's _glory_ that shines through our _~~goodness~~ broken_ pieces.

1 Peter 1:7

God's _~~power~~ goodness/glory_ is revealed when we walk with Him and trust in Him.

Isaiah 61:3

Video Viewer Guide Answers

Week 1
Scorekeeping
Helicoptering
Interrupting
Nagging
Excessive Planning
always
Believe
all / hard
Challenge
others / outcomes

Week 2
faith / feelings
priorities / plans
Jesus / satisfy

Week 3
truth / lies
timeline
let go

Week 4
happiness / God
worshiping God / eternal impact
personally
Hula-Hoop
think
bless /stress

Week 5
Pray(ing)
Forgiving
hope / heartache
stop / pray

Week 6
power / peace / provision
heart
mind
hands
perfection
holds / together
glory
goodness

Notes

Week 1

1. Wikipedia, s.v., "smash cut," last modified December 1, 2019, https://en.wikipedia.org/wiki/Smash_cut.
2. Bible Atlas, s.v., "Wilderness of Judea," https://bibleatlas.org/wilderness_of_judea.htm, accessed June 25, 2019.
3. Ronald F. Youngblood, *Nelson's Illustrated Bible Dictionary: New and Enhanced Edition* (Nashville: Thomas Nelson, 2014), 1188.
4. Bible Hub, s.v. "Mark 1:13," https://biblehub.com/commentaries/mark/1-13.htm., accessed February 5, 2020.
5. Youngblood, *Nelson's Illustrated Bible Dictionary*, 1188.
6. Mike Mason, *The Gospel According to Job: An Honest Look at Pain and Doubt from the Life of One Who Lost Everything* (Wheaton, IL: Crossway Books, 1994), 152.
7. Todd Hunter, "Our Top Five Temptations," https://www.faithgateway.com/our-top-five-temptations/, accessed February 5, 2020.
8. Hunter, "Our Top Five Temptations."
9. Warren W. Wiersbe, *The Wiersbe Bible Commentary: New Testament* (Colorado Springs, CO: David C. Cook, 2007), 16.
10. Youngblood, *Nelson's Illustrated Bible Dictionary*, 515.
11. Warren W. Wiersbe, *The Wiersbe Bible Commentary: Old Testament* (Colorado Springs, CO: David C. Cook, 2007), 151.
12. Bible Hub, s.v. "kalos," https://biblehub.com/greek/2570.htm, accessed February 2, 2020.

Week 2

1. *The ESV Study Bible* (Wheaton, IL: Crossway, 2008), 1825.
2. Randall C. Zachman, *John Calvin as Teacher, Pastor, and Theologian: The Shape of his Writings and Thought* (Grand Rapids: Baker Academic, 2006), paraphrased, 224.

3. Bible Hub, s.v. "zéteó," https://biblehub.com/greek/2212.htm, accessed July 12, 2019.
4. Wiersbe, *The Wiersbe Bible Commentary: Old Testament*, 825.
5. Wiersbe, *The Wiersbe Bible Commentary: New Testament*, 148.
6. *The ESV Study Bible* (Wheaton, IL: Crossway, 2008), 1825.
7. E. Ray Clendenen and Jeremy Royal Howard, eds., "Numbers 11:5-6," *Holman Illustrated Bible Commentary* (Nashville: B&H Publishing Group, 2015), 144.
8. Ronald F. Youngblood. *Nelson's Illustrated Bible Dictionary: New and Enhanced Edition* (Nashville: Thomas Nelson, 2014), 65.
9. Ann Voskamp, *One Thousand Gifts: A Dare to Live Fully Right Where You Are* (Grand Rapids, MI: Zondervan, 2010), 15.
10. Youngblood, *Nelson's Illustrated Bible Dictionary*, 65.
11. Clendenen and Howard, *Holman Illustrated Bible Commentary*, 145.
12. Maria Newman and Christine Hauser, "Astronaut Charged with Attempted Murder," *New York Times*, February 6, 2007, https://www.nytimes.com/2007/02/06/us/06cnd-astronaut.html, accessed on August 26, 2019.
13. Stacey Nguyen, "Lucy in the Sky: Here Is Former Astronaut Lisa Nowak's Status after Her 2007 Scandal," Popsugar, March 29, 2019, https://www.popsugar.com/entertainment/Where-Lisa-Nowak-Now-2019-45941897, accessed August 26, 2019.
14. Chip Dodd, *The Voice of the Heart: A Call to Full Living* (Nashville: Sage Hill, LLC, 2004), loc 93.
15. Dodd, loc 275.
16. Alan S. Cowen and Dacher Keltner, "Self-report Captures 27 Distinct Categories of Emotion Bridged by Continuous Gradients," PNAS, https://www.pnas.org/content/early/2017/08/30/1702247114, accessed on August 26, 2019.
17. Dodd, loc 542.
18. Bible Hub, s.v. "Leb," https://biblehub.com/hebrew/3820.htm, accessed August 26, 2019.
19. Bible Hub, s.v. "Shaken," https://biblehub.com/hebrew/7931.htm, accessed August 26, 2019.
20. Wiersbe, *The Wiersbe Bible Commentary, Old Testament*, 182.
21. Youngblood, *Nelson's Illustrated Bible Dictionary*, 402.
22. Clinton E. Arnold, gen. ed., *Zondervan Illustrated Bible Backgrounds Commentary, Volume 2: John, Acts* (Grand Rapids, MI: Zondervan, 2002), 78.
23. Bible Hub, s.v. "nephesh," https://biblehub.com/hebrew/5315.htm, accessed August 15, 2019.

Week 3

1. Wiersbe, *The Wiersbe Bible Commentary: New Testament*, 148.
2. Youngblood, *Nelson's Illustrated Bible Dictionary*, 1114.
3. Youngblood, *Nelson's Illustrated Bible Dictionary*, 1115.
4. Wiersbe, *Wiersbe Bible Commentary: New Testament*, 148.

5. Clendenden and Howard, *Holman Illustrated Bible Commentary*, 184.

6. David Guzik, "How to Judge an Apostle," https://www.blueletterbible.org/Comm/guzik_david/StudyGuide2017-2Cr/2Cr-10.cfm, accessed February 3, 2020.

7. Clinton E. Arnold, gen. ed., *Zondervan Illustrated Bible Backgrounds Commentary*, Volume 3: *Romans to Philemon* (Grand Rapids, MI: Zondervan, 2002), 239.

8. Arnold, *Zondervan Illustrated Bible Backgrounds Commentary*: Volume 3: *Romans to Philemon*, 240.

9. Jill Savage, *Empty Nest, Full Life: Discovering God's Best for Your Next* (Chicago: Moody Publishers, 2019), 62.

10. Savage, *Empty Nest, Full Life*, 63.

11. Savage, *Empty Nest, Full Life*, 65.

Week 4

1. Cristiano Ronaldo, "No doubts in your mind, no dandruff on your head," Facebook, August 27, 2019, https://www.facebook.com/Cristiano/, accessed on August 27, 2019.

2. Rick Warren, *The Purpose Driven Life: What on Earth Am I Here For?* expanded edition (Grand Rapids, MI: Zondervan, 2012), 23.

3. "Matthew Henry's Concise Commentary," s.v. Matthew 4:8, https://biblehub.com/commentaries/matthew/4-8.htm, accessed on August 27, 2019.

4. David Guzik, "Matthew 4—The Temptation of Jesus and His First Galilean Ministry," https://enduringword.com/bible-commentary/matthew-4/, accessed July 21, 2019.

5. Warren, *The Purpose Driven Life*, 190.

6. Rick Warren, "Purpose Driven Life Author Rick Warren on Open House," https://hope1032.com.au/stories/faith/christian-living/2013/purpose-driven-life-author-rick-warren-on-open-house/, interview by Leigh Hatcher, hope 103.2, February 8, 2013, accessed August 28, 2019.

7. Clendenden and Howard, *Holman Illustrated Bible Commentary*, 1010.

8. Tim Keller, "The Prodigal God-The Elder Brother," https://www.youtube.com/watch?v=OasF7lWlX_M, accessed August 28, 2019.

9. Wiersbe, *Wiersbe Bible Commentary*: Old Testament, 319.

10. Wiersbe, *Wiersbe Bible Commentary*: Old Testament, 200.

11. Clendenden and Howard, *Holman Illustrated Bible Commentary*, 102.

12. Psychologytoday.com "10 Signs You're a People-Pleaser" – accessed July 23, 2019

13. *The ESV Study Bible* (Wheaton, IL: Crossway, 2008), 2269.

14. Clendenden and Howard, *Holman Illustrated Bible Commentary*, 102.

15. Clendenden and Howard, *Holman Illustrated Bible Commentary*, 102.

16. Kathi Lipp, *Clutter Free: Quick and Easy Steps to Simplifying Your Space* (Eugene, OR: Harvest House, 2015), 77.

17. Lipp, *Clutter Free*, 78.

18. Wiersbe, *Wiersbe Bible Commentary*: New Testament, 24.

19. Dietrich Bonhoeffer, *The Cost of Discipleship* (New York: Macmillan, 1959), 174.

20. Andy Stanley, *How to Be Rich: It's Not What You Have, It's What You Do with What You Have* (Grand Rapids, MI: Zondervan, 2013), Loc 1139.

Week 5

1. "History of Hymns: 'I Surrender All,'" https://www.umcdiscipleship.org/resources/history-of-hymns-i-surrender-all, accessed February 3, 2020.
2. "History of Hymns: 'I Surrender All.'"
3. Wiersbe, *Wiersbe Bible Commentary: New Testament*, 16.
4. Wiersbe, *Wiersbe Bible Commentary: New Testament*, 113.
5. Wiersbe, *Wiersbe Bible Commentary: New Testament*, 113.
6. Youngblood, *Nelson's Illustrated Bible Dictionary*, 1208.
7. Youngblood, *Nelson's Illustrated Bible Dictionary*, 49.
8. Al-Anon Family Group Head Inc., *Courage to Change: One Day at a Time in Al-Anon* (Virginia Beach, VA: Al Anon Family Group Headquarters, 1992), 48.
9. Martin Luther, *A Simple Way to Pray* (Louisville: Westminster John Knox, 2000), 18.
10. Janet Holm McHenry. *The Complete Guide to the Prayers of Jesus: What Jesus Prayed and How It Can Change Your Life Today* (Bloomington, MN: Bethany House, 2018), 55.
11. McHenry, *The Complete Guide to the Prayers of Jesus*, 12.
12. Clinton E. Arnold, gen. ed., *Zondervan Illustrated Bible Backgrounds Commentary*, Volume 3: *Matthew, Mark, Luke* (Grand Rapids, MI: Zondervan, 2002), 166.
13. Wiersbe, *Wiersbe Bible Commentary: New Testament*, 216.
14. Anne Lamott, *Help, Thanks, Wow: The Three Essential Prayers* (New York: Penguin, 2012), 35.
15. Barb Roose, *Winning the Worry Battle* (Nashville: Abingdon Press, 2018), 20.
16. Art of Manliness (podcast), "#527: Father Wounds, Male Spirituality, and the Journey to the Second Half of Life,"https://podcasts.apple.com/us/podcast/527-father-wounds-male-spirituality-journey-to-second/id332516054?i=1000445071229.
17. Art of Manliness.
18. "Things that Matter: Rick Warren on the Unexpected Success of The Purpose Driven Life," https://www.youtube.com/watch?v=IjejJbRLfDM, accessed August 27, 2019.
19. "History of Hymns: 'It Is Well with My Soul,'" https://www.umcdiscipleship.org/resources/history-of-hymns-it-is-well-with-my-soul, accessed February 4, 2020.

Week 6

1. Stefano Carnazzi, "*Kintsugi*: The Art of Precious Scars," Lifegate, https://www.lifegate.com/people/lifestyle/kintsugi, accessed August 7, 2019.
2. Toni King, "Pacific Northwest Upcycling and Ancient Japanese Kintsukuroi," Hammer & Hand, April 22, 2013, https://hammerandhand.com/field-notes/pacific-northwest-upcycling-ancient-japanese-kintsukuroi/, accessed February 4, 2020.
3. Youngblood, *Nelson's Illustrated Bible Dictionary*, 758.